HOUSE CHECKLIST

CW00448103

BUY THE HOUSE THAT TICKS ALL THE BOXES

Tahir Yaqub

YOUR GUIDE TO BUYING A HOUSE

When buying a house, it is important that you take into account all the important factors and don't miss anything. The best way to achieve this is by using a checklist for every house you visit with an intention to buy.

This checklist is designed for this specific purpose. This will guide you to tick more than 60 checkboxes for every house you look for buying. There are about 100 pages which should be more than enough for you to make an informed decision. However, don't forget this to take with you!

Address _____   Price _____

Bedrooms _____   Bathrooms _____   Sq.Ft. _____

Lot Size: _____   Year Built _____   School District _____

Annual Tax _____

EXTERIOR

	Good	Average	Poor
View/Yard/Landscaping	☐	☐	☐
Trees	☐	☐	☐
Lawn (Front)	☐	☐	☐
Lawn (Back)	☐	☐	☐
Fences (condition)	☐	☐	☐
Landscaping (condition)	☐	☐	☐
Irrigation / Sprinkler	☐	☐	☐
	☐	☐	☐
House Type	☐	☐	☐
Exterior Siding	☐	☐	☐
Deck / Patio / Porch	☐	☐	☐
Garage	☐	☐	☐
Window / Doors	☐	☐	☐
Roof / Gutters	☐	☐	☐
Fencing	☐	☐	☐

HOME SYSTEMS

	Good	Average	Poor
Electrical	☐	☐	☐
Air Conditioning / Fans	☐	☐	☐
Heating	☐	☐	☐
Security	☐	☐	☐
Plumbing	☐	☐	☐
Intercom	☐	☐	☐

FEATURES

	Good	Average	Poor
Home Warranty	☐	☐	☐
Energy Saving Features	☐	☐	☐

INTERIOR

	Good	Average	Poor
Walls / Trim / Ceilings	☐	☐	☐
Flooring	☐	☐	☐
Stairs	☐	☐	☐
Storage	☐	☐	☐
Living Room	☐	☐	☐
Family Room	☐	☐	☐
Dining Room	☐	☐	☐

	Good	Average	Poor
Master Bedroom	☐	☐	☐
Bedroom 2	☐	☐	☐
Bedroom 3	☐	☐	☐
Bedroom 4	☐	☐	☐
Master Bathroom	☐	☐	☐
Bathroom 2	☐	☐	☐
Bathroom 3	☐	☐	☐
Bonus / Game Room	☐	☐	☐

	Good	Average	Poor
Kitchen	☐	☐	☐
Cabinets	☐	☐	☐
Countertop	☐	☐	☐
Counter Space	☐	☐	☐
Flooring	☐	☐	☐
Oven / Stove	☐	☐	☐
Microwave	☐	☐	☐
Layout	☐	☐	☐
Light Fixtures	☐	☐	☐
Backsplash	☐	☐	☐
Pantry	☐	☐	☐
Appliances	☐	☐	☐
Island	☐	☐	☐

	Good	Average	Poor
Basement	☐	☐	☐
Garage	☐	☐	☐

COMMUNITY

	Good	Average	Poor
Immediate Neighborhood	☐	☐	☐
Close to Employment	☐	☐	☐
Close to Shopping	☐	☐	☐
Close to Transportation	☐	☐	☐
Close to Schools / Daycare	☐	☐	☐
Close to Places of Worship	☐	☐	☐
Near Recreational Facilities	☐	☐	☐
Close to Airport	☐	☐	☐
Near Police and Fire Department	☐	☐	☐

Address _____ Price _____

Bedrooms _____ Bathrooms _____ Sq.Ft. _____

Lot Size: _____ Year Built _____ School District _____

Annual Tax _____

EXTERIOR

	Good	Average	Poor
View/Yard/Landscaping	☐	☐	☐
Trees	☐	☐	☐
Lawn (Front)	☐	☐	☐
Lawn (Back)	☐	☐	☐
Fences (condition)	☐	☐	☐
Landscaping (condition)	☐	☐	☐
Irrigation / Sprinkler	☐	☐	☐
	☐	☐	☐
House Type	☐	☐	☐
Exterior Siding	☐	☐	☐
Deck / Patio / Porch	☐	☐	☐
Garage	☐	☐	☐
Window / Doors	☐	☐	☐
Roof / Gutters	☐	☐	☐
Fencing	☐	☐	☐

HOME SYSTEMS

	Good	Average	Poor
Electrical	☐	☐	☐
Air Conditioning / Fans	☐	☐	☐
Heating	☐	☐	☐
Security	☐	☐	☐
Plumbing	☐	☐	☐
Intercom	☐	☐	☐

FEATURES

	Good	Average	Poor
Home Warranty	☐	☐	☐
Energy Saving Features	☐	☐	☐

INTERIOR

	Good	Average	Poor
Walls / Trim / Ceilings	☐	☐	☐
Flooring	☐	☐	☐
Stairs	☐	☐	☐
Storage	☐	☐	☐
Living Room	☐	☐	☐
Family Room	☐	☐	☐
Dining Room	☐	☐	☐

	Good	Average	Poor
Master Bedroom	☐	☐	☐
Bedroom 2	☐	☐	☐
Bedroom 3	☐	☐	☐
Bedroom 4	☐	☐	☐
Master Bathroom	☐	☐	☐
Bathroom 2	☐	☐	☐
Bathroom 3	☐	☐	☐
Bonus / Game Room	☐	☐	☐

	Good	Average	Poor
Kitchen	☐	☐	☐
Cabinets	☐	☐	☐
Countertop	☐	☐	☐
Counter Space	☐	☐	☐
Flooring	☐	☐	☐
Oven / Stove	☐	☐	☐
Microwave	☐	☐	☐
Layout	☐	☐	☐
Light Fixtures	☐	☐	☐
Backsplash	☐	☐	☐
Pantry	☐	☐	☐
Appliances	☐	☐	☐
Island	☐	☐	☐

	Good	Average	Poor
Basement	☐	☐	☐
Garage	☐	☐	☐

COMMUNITY

	Good	Average	Poor
Immediate Neighborhood	☐	☐	☐
Close to Employment	☐	☐	☐
Close to Shopping	☐	☐	☐
Close to Transportation	☐	☐	☐
Close to Schools / Daycare	☐	☐	☐
Close to Places of Worship	☐	☐	☐
Near Recreational Facilities	☐	☐	☐
Close to Airport	☐	☐	☐
Near Police and Fire Department	☐	☐	☐

Address _____ Price _____

Bedrooms _____ Bathrooms _____ Sq.Ft. _____

Lot Size: _____ Year Built _____ School District _____

Annual Tax _____

EXTERIOR

	Good	Average	Poor
View/Yard/Landscaping	☐	☐	☐
Trees	☐	☐	☐
Lawn (Front)	☐	☐	☐
Lawn (Back)	☐	☐	☐
Fences (condition)	☐	☐	☐
Landscaping (condition)	☐	☐	☐
Irrigation / Sprinkler	☐	☐	☐
	☐	☐	☐
House Type	☐	☐	☐
Exterior Siding	☐	☐	☐
Deck / Patio / Porch	☐	☐	☐
Garage	☐	☐	☐
Window / Doors	☐	☐	☐
Roof / Gutters	☐	☐	☐
Fencing	☐	☐	☐

	Good	Average	Poor
Master Bedroom	☐	☐	☐
Bedroom 2	☐	☐	☐
Bedroom 3	☐	☐	☐
Bedroom 4	☐	☐	☐
Master Bathroom	☐	☐	☐
Bathroom 2	☐	☐	☐
Bathroom 3	☐	☐	☐
Bonus / Game Room	☐	☐	☐

	Good	Average	Poor
Kitchen	☐	☐	☐
Cabinets	☐	☐	☐
Countertop	☐	☐	☐
Counter Space	☐	☐	☐
Flooring	☐	☐	☐
Oven / Stove	☐	☐	☐
Microwave	☐	☐	☐
Layout	☐	☐	☐
Light Fixtures	☐	☐	☐
Backsplash	☐	☐	☐
Pantry	☐	☐	☐
Appliances	☐	☐	☐
Island	☐	☐	☐

	Good	Average	Poor
Basement	☐	☐	☐
Garage	☐	☐	☐

HOME SYSTEMS

	Good	Average	Poor
Electrical	☐	☐	☐
Air Conditioning / Fans	☐	☐	☐
Heating	☐	☐	☐
Security	☐	☐	☐
Plumbing	☐	☐	☐
Intercom	☐	☐	☐

FEATURES

	Good	Average	Poor
Home Warranty	☐	☐	☐
Energy Saving Features	☐	☐	☐

INTERIOR

	Good	Average	Poor
Walls / Trim / Ceilings	☐	☐	☐
Flooring	☐	☐	☐
Stairs	☐	☐	☐
Storage	☐	☐	☐
Living Room	☐	☐	☐
Family Room	☐	☐	☐
Dining Room	☐	☐	☐

COMMUNITY

	Good	Average	Poor
Immediate Neighborhood	☐	☐	☐
Close to Employment	☐	☐	☐
Close to Shopping	☐	☐	☐
Close to Transportation	☐	☐	☐
Close to Schools / Daycare	☐	☐	☐
Close to Places of Worship	☐	☐	☐
Near Recreational Facilities	☐	☐	☐
Close to Airport	☐	☐	☐
Near Police and Fire Department	☐	☐	☐

Address _____ Price _____

Bedrooms _____ Bathrooms _____ Sq.Ft. _____

Lot Size: _____ Year Built _____ School District _____

Annual Tax _____

EXTERIOR

	Good	Average	Poor
View/Yard/Landscaping	☐	☐	☐
Trees	☐	☐	☐
Lawn (Front)	☐	☐	☐
Lawn (Back)	☐	☐	☐
Fences (condition)	☐	☐	☐
Landscaping (condition)	☐	☐	☐
Irrigation / Sprinkler	☐	☐	☐
	☐	☐	☐
House Type	☐	☐	☐
Exterior Siding	☐	☐	☐
Deck / Patio / Porch	☐	☐	☐
Garage	☐	☐	☐
Window / Doors	☐	☐	☐
Roof / Gutters	☐	☐	☐
Fencing	☐	☐	☐

HOME SYSTEMS

	Good	Average	Poor
Electrical	☐	☐	☐
Air Conditioning / Fans	☐	☐	☐
Heating	☐	☐	☐
Security	☐	☐	☐
Plumbing	☐	☐	☐
Intercom	☐	☐	☐

FEATURES

	Good	Average	Poor
Home Warranty	☐	☐	☐
Energy Saving Features	☐	☐	☐

INTERIOR

	Good	Average	Poor
Walls / Trim / Ceilings	☐	☐	☐
Flooring	☐	☐	☐
Stairs	☐	☐	☐
Storage	☐	☐	☐
Living Room	☐	☐	☐
Family Room	☐	☐	☐
Dining Room	☐	☐	☐

	Good	Average	Poor
Master Bedroom	☐	☐	☐
Bedroom 2	☐	☐	☐
Bedroom 3	☐	☐	☐
Bedroom 4	☐	☐	☐
Master Bathroom	☐	☐	☐
Bathroom 2	☐	☐	☐
Bathroom 3	☐	☐	☐
Bonus / Game Room	☐	☐	☐

	Good	Average	Poor
Kitchen	☐	☐	☐
Cabinets	☐	☐	☐
Countertop	☐	☐	☐
Counter Space	☐	☐	☐
Flooring	☐	☐	☐
Oven / Stove	☐	☐	☐
Microwave	☐	☐	☐
Layout	☐	☐	☐
Light Fixtures	☐	☐	☐
Backsplash	☐	☐	☐
Pantry	☐	☐	☐
Appliances	☐	☐	☐
Island	☐	☐	☐

	Good	Average	Poor
Basement	☐	☐	☐
Garage	☐	☐	☐

COMMUNITY

	Good	Average	Poor
Immediate Neighborhood	☐	☐	☐
Close to Employment	☐	☐	☐
Close to Shopping	☐	☐	☐
Close to Transportation	☐	☐	☐
Close to Schools / Daycare	☐	☐	☐
Close to Places of Worship	☐	☐	☐
Near Recreational Facilities	☐	☐	☐
Close to Airport	☐	☐	☐
Near Police and Fire Department	☐	☐	☐

8

Address _____   Price _____

Bedrooms _____   Bathrooms _____   Sq.Ft. _____

Lot Size: _____   Year Built _____   School District _____

Annual Tax _____

EXTERIOR

	Good	Average	Poor
View/Yard/Landscaping	☐	☐	☐
Trees	☐	☐	☐
Lawn (Front)	☐	☐	☐
Lawn (Back)	☐	☐	☐
Fences (condition)	☐	☐	☐
Landscaping (condition)	☐	☐	☐
Irrigation / Sprinkler	☐	☐	☐
	☐	☐	☐
House Type	☐	☐	☐
Exterior Siding	☐	☐	☐
Deck / Patio / Porch	☐	☐	☐
Garage	☐	☐	☐
Window / Doors	☐	☐	☐
Roof / Gutters	☐	☐	☐
Fencing	☐	☐	☐

HOME SYSTEMS

	Good	Average	Poor
Electrical	☐	☐	☐
Air Conditioning / Fans	☐	☐	☐
Heating	☐	☐	☐
Security	☐	☐	☐
Plumbing	☐	☐	☐
Intercom	☐	☐	☐

FEATURES

	Good	Average	Poor
Home Warranty	☐	☐	☐
Energy Saving Features	☐	☐	☐

INTERIOR

	Good	Average	Poor
Walls / Trim / Ceilings	☐	☐	☐
Flooring	☐	☐	☐
Stairs	☐	☐	☐
Storage	☐	☐	☐
Living Room	☐	☐	☐
Family Room	☐	☐	☐
Dining Room	☐	☐	☐

	Good	Average	Poor
Master Bedroom	☐	☐	☐
Bedroom 2	☐	☐	☐
Bedroom 3	☐	☐	☐
Bedroom 4	☐	☐	☐
Master Bathroom	☐	☐	☐
Bathroom 2	☐	☐	☐
Bathroom 3	☐	☐	☐
Bonus / Game Room	☐	☐	☐

	Good	Average	Poor
Kitchen	☐	☐	☐
Cabinets	☐	☐	☐
Countertop	☐	☐	☐
Counter Space	☐	☐	☐
Flooring	☐	☐	☐
Oven / Stove	☐	☐	☐
Microwave	☐	☐	☐
Layout	☐	☐	☐
Light Fixtures	☐	☐	☐
Backsplash	☐	☐	☐
Pantry	☐	☐	☐
Appliances	☐	☐	☐
Island	☐	☐	☐

	Good	Average	Poor
Basement	☐	☐	☐
Garage	☐	☐	☐

COMMUNITY

	Good	Average	Poor
Immediate Neighborhood	☐	☐	☐
Close to Employment	☐	☐	☐
Close to Shopping	☐	☐	☐
Close to Transportation	☐	☐	☐
Close to Schools / Daycare	☐	☐	☐
Close to Places of Worship	☐	☐	☐
Near Recreational Facilities	☐	☐	☐
Close to Airport	☐	☐	☐
Near Police and Fire Department	☐	☐	☐

9

Address _____   Price _____

Bedrooms _____   Bathrooms _____   Sq.Ft. _____

Lot Size: _____   Year Built _____   School District _____

Annual Tax _____

EXTERIOR

	Good	Average	Poor
View/Yard/Landscaping	☐	☐	☐
Trees	☐	☐	☐
Lawn (Front)	☐	☐	☐
Lawn (Back)	☐	☐	☐
Fences (condition)	☐	☐	☐
Landscaping (condition)	☐	☐	☐
Irrigation / Sprinkler	☐	☐	☐
	☐	☐	☐
House Type	☐	☐	☐
Exterior Siding	☐	☐	☐
Deck / Patio / Porch	☐	☐	☐
Garage	☐	☐	☐
Window / Doors	☐	☐	☐
Roof / Gutters	☐	☐	☐
Fencing	☐	☐	☐

HOME SYSTEMS

	Good	Average	Poor
Electrical	☐	☐	☐
Air Conditioning / Fans	☐	☐	☐
Heating	☐	☐	☐
Security	☐	☐	☐
Plumbing	☐	☐	☐
Intercom	☐	☐	☐

FEATURES

	Good	Average	Poor
Home Warranty	☐	☐	☐
Energy Saving Features	☐	☐	☐

INTERIOR

	Good	Average	Poor
Walls / Trim / Ceilings	☐	☐	☐
Flooring	☐	☐	☐
Stairs	☐	☐	☐
Storage	☐	☐	☐
Living Room	☐	☐	☐
Family Room	☐	☐	☐
Dining Room	☐	☐	☐

	Good	Average	Poor
Master Bedroom	☐	☐	☐
Bedroom 2	☐	☐	☐
Bedroom 3	☐	☐	☐
Bedroom 4	☐	☐	☐
Master Bathroom	☐	☐	☐
Bathroom 2	☐	☐	☐
Bathroom 3	☐	☐	☐
Bonus / Game Room	☐	☐	☐

	Good	Average	Poor
Kitchen	☐	☐	☐
Cabinets	☐	☐	☐
Countertop	☐	☐	☐
Counter Space	☐	☐	☐
Flooring	☐	☐	☐
Oven / Stove	☐	☐	☐
Microwave	☐	☐	☐
Layout	☐	☐	☐
Light Fixtures	☐	☐	☐
Backsplash	☐	☐	☐
Pantry	☐	☐	☐
Appliances	☐	☐	☐
Island	☐	☐	☐

	Good	Average	Poor
Basement	☐	☐	☐
Garage	☐	☐	☐

COMMUNITY

	Good	Average	Poor
Immediate Neighborhood	☐	☐	☐
Close to Employment	☐	☐	☐
Close to Shopping	☐	☐	☐
Close to Transportation	☐	☐	☐
Close to Schools / Daycare	☐	☐	☐
Close to Places of Worship	☐	☐	☐
Near Recreational Facilities	☐	☐	☐
Close to Airport	☐	☐	☐
Near Police and Fire Department	☐	☐	☐

Address _____ Price _____

Bedrooms _____ Bathrooms _____ Sq.Ft. _____

Lot Size: _____ Year Built _____ School District _____

Annual Tax _____

EXTERIOR

	Good	Average	Poor
View/Yard/Landscaping	☐	☐	☐
Trees	☐	☐	☐
Lawn (Front)	☐	☐	☐
Lawn (Back)	☐	☐	☐
Fences (condition)	☐	☐	☐
Landscaping (condition)	☐	☐	☐
Irrigation / Sprinkler	☐	☐	☐
	☐	☐	☐
House Type	☐	☐	☐
Exterior Siding	☐	☐	☐
Deck / Patio / Porch	☐	☐	☐
Garage	☐	☐	☐
Window / Doors	☐	☐	☐
Roof / Gutters	☐	☐	☐
Fencing	☐	☐	☐

HOME SYSTEMS

	Good	Average	Poor
Electrical	☐	☐	☐
Air Conditioning / Fans	☐	☐	☐
Heating	☐	☐	☐
Security	☐	☐	☐
Plumbing	☐	☐	☐
Intercom	☐	☐	☐

FEATURES

	Good	Average	Poor
Home Warranty	☐	☐	☐
Energy Saving Features	☐	☐	☐

INTERIOR

	Good	Average	Poor
Walls / Trim / Ceilings	☐	☐	☐
Flooring	☐	☐	☐
Stairs	☐	☐	☐
Storage	☐	☐	☐
Living Room	☐	☐	☐
Family Room	☐	☐	☐
Dining Room	☐	☐	☐

	Good	Average	Poor
Master Bedroom	☐	☐	☐
Bedroom 2	☐	☐	☐
Bedroom 3	☐	☐	☐
Bedroom 4	☐	☐	☐
Master Bathroom	☐	☐	☐
Bathroom 2	☐	☐	☐
Bathroom 3	☐	☐	☐
Bonus / Game Room	☐	☐	☐

	Good	Average	Poor
Kitchen	☐	☐	☐
Cabinets	☐	☐	☐
Countertop	☐	☐	☐
Counter Space	☐	☐	☐
Flooring	☐	☐	☐
Oven / Stove	☐	☐	☐
Microwave	☐	☐	☐
Layout	☐	☐	☐
Light Fixtures	☐	☐	☐
Backsplash	☐	☐	☐
Pantry	☐	☐	☐
Appliances	☐	☐	☐
Island	☐	☐	☐

	Good	Average	Poor
Basement	☐	☐	☐
Garage	☐	☐	☐

COMMUNITY

	Good	Average	Poor
Immediate Neighborhood	☐	☐	☐
Close to Employment	☐	☐	☐
Close to Shopping	☐	☐	☐
Close to Transportation	☐	☐	☐
Close to Schools / Daycare	☐	☐	☐
Close to Places of Worship	☐	☐	☐
Near Recreational Facilities	☐	☐	☐
Close to Airport	☐	☐	☐
Near Police and Fire Department	☐	☐	☐

11

Address _____   Price _____

Bedrooms _____   Bathrooms _____   Sq.Ft. _____

Lot Size: _____   Year Built _____   School District _____

Annual Tax _____

EXTERIOR

	Good	Average	Poor
View/Yard/Landscaping	☐	☐	☐
Trees	☐	☐	☐
Lawn (Front)	☐	☐	☐
Lawn (Back)	☐	☐	☐
Fences (condition)	☐	☐	☐
Landscaping (condition)	☐	☐	☐
Irrigation / Sprinkler	☐	☐	☐
	☐	☐	☐
House Type	☐	☐	☐
Exterior Siding	☐	☐	☐
Deck / Patio / Porch	☐	☐	☐
Garage	☐	☐	☐
Window / Doors	☐	☐	☐
Roof / Gutters	☐	☐	☐
Fencing	☐	☐	☐

HOME SYSTEMS

	Good	Average	Poor
Electrical	☐	☐	☐
Air Conditioning / Fans	☐	☐	☐
Heating	☐	☐	☐
Security	☐	☐	☐
Plumbing	☐	☐	☐
Intercom	☐	☐	☐

FEATURES

	Good	Average	Poor
Home Warranty	☐	☐	☐
Energy Saving Features	☐	☐	☐

INTERIOR

	Good	Average	Poor
Walls / Trim / Ceilings	☐	☐	☐
Flooring	☐	☐	☐
Stairs	☐	☐	☐
Storage	☐	☐	☐
Living Room	☐	☐	☐
Family Room	☐	☐	☐
Dining Room	☐	☐	☐

	Good	Average	Poor
Master Bedroom	☐	☐	☐
Bedroom 2	☐	☐	☐
Bedroom 3	☐	☐	☐
Bedroom 4	☐	☐	☐
Master Bathroom	☐	☐	☐
Bathroom 2	☐	☐	☐
Bathroom 3	☐	☐	☐
Bonus / Game Room	☐	☐	☐

	Good	Average	Poor
Kitchen	☐	☐	☐
Cabinets	☐	☐	☐
Countertop	☐	☐	☐
Counter Space	☐	☐	☐
Flooring	☐	☐	☐
Oven / Stove	☐	☐	☐
Microwave	☐	☐	☐
Layout	☐	☐	☐
Light Fixtures	☐	☐	☐
Backsplash	☐	☐	☐
Pantry	☐	☐	☐
Appliances	☐	☐	☐
Island	☐	☐	☐

	Good	Average	Poor
Basement	☐	☐	☐
Garage	☐	☐	☐

COMMUNITY

	Good	Average	Poor
Immediate Neighborhood	☐	☐	☐
Close to Employment	☐	☐	☐
Close to Shopping	☐	☐	☐
Close to Transportation	☐	☐	☐
Close to Schools / Daycare	☐	☐	☐
Close to Places of Worship	☐	☐	☐
Near Recreational Facilities	☐	☐	☐
Close to Airport	☐	☐	☐
Near Police and Fire Department	☐	☐	☐

Address _____ Price _____

Bedrooms _____ Bathrooms _____ Sq.Ft. _____

Lot Size: _____ Year Built _____ School District _____

Annual Tax _____

EXTERIOR

	Good	Average	Poor
View/Yard/Landscaping	☐	☐	☐
Trees	☐	☐	☐
Lawn (Front)	☐	☐	☐
Lawn (Back)	☐	☐	☐
Fences (condition)	☐	☐	☐
Landscaping (condition)	☐	☐	☐
Irrigation / Sprinkler	☐	☐	☐
	☐	☐	☐
House Type	☐	☐	☐
Exterior Siding	☐	☐	☐
Deck / Patio / Porch	☐	☐	☐
Garage	☐	☐	☐
Window / Doors	☐	☐	☐
Roof / Gutters	☐	☐	☐
Fencing	☐	☐	☐

	Good	Average	Poor
Master Bedroom	☐	☐	☐
Bedroom 2	☐	☐	☐
Bedroom 3	☐	☐	☐
Bedroom 4	☐	☐	☐
Master Bathroom	☐	☐	☐
Bathroom 2	☐	☐	☐
Bathroom 3	☐	☐	☐
Bonus / Game Room	☐	☐	☐

	Good	Average	Poor
Kitchen	☐	☐	☐
Cabinets	☐	☐	☐
Countertop	☐	☐	☐
Counter Space	☐	☐	☐
Flooring	☐	☐	☐
Oven / Stove	☐	☐	☐
Microwave	☐	☐	☐
Layout	☐	☐	☐
Light Fixtures	☐	☐	☐
Backsplash	☐	☐	☐
Pantry	☐	☐	☐
Appliances	☐	☐	☐
Island	☐	☐	☐

	Good	Average	Poor
Basement	☐	☐	☐
Garage	☐	☐	☐

HOME SYSTEMS

	Good	Average	Poor
Electrical	☐	☐	☐
Air Conditioning / Fans	☐	☐	☐
Heating	☐	☐	☐
Security	☐	☐	☐
Plumbing	☐	☐	☐
Intercom	☐	☐	☐

FEATURES

	Good	Average	Poor
Home Warranty	☐	☐	☐
Energy Saving Features	☐	☐	☐

INTERIOR

	Good	Average	Poor
Walls / Trim / Ceilings	☐	☐	☐
Flooring	☐	☐	☐
Stairs	☐	☐	☐
Storage	☐	☐	☐
Living Room	☐	☐	☐
Family Room	☐	☐	☐
Dining Room	☐	☐	☐

COMMUNITY

	Good	Average	Poor
Immediate Neighborhood	☐	☐	☐
Close to Employment	☐	☐	☐
Close to Shopping	☐	☐	☐
Close to Transportation	☐	☐	☐
Close to Schools / Daycare	☐	☐	☐
Close to Places of Worship	☐	☐	☐
Near Recreational Facilities	☐	☐	☐
Close to Airport	☐	☐	☐
Near Police and Fire Department	☐	☐	☐

Address _____ Price _____

Bedrooms _____ Bathrooms _____ Sq.Ft. _____

Lot Size: _____ Year Built _____ School District _____

Annual Tax _____

EXTERIOR

	Good	Average	Poor
View/Yard/Landscaping	☐	☐	☐
Trees	☐	☐	☐
Lawn (Front)	☐	☐	☐
Lawn (Back)	☐	☐	☐
Fences (condition)	☐	☐	☐
Landscaping (condition)	☐	☐	☐
Irrigation / Sprinkler	☐	☐	☐
	☐	☐	☐
House Type	☐	☐	☐
Exterior Siding	☐	☐	☐
Deck / Patio / Porch	☐	☐	☐
Garage	☐	☐	☐
Window / Doors	☐	☐	☐
Roof / Gutters	☐	☐	☐
Fencing	☐	☐	☐

HOME SYSTEMS

	Good	Average	Poor
Electrical	☐	☐	☐
Air Conditioning / Fans	☐	☐	☐
Heating	☐	☐	☐
Security	☐	☐	☐
Plumbing	☐	☐	☐
Intercom	☐	☐	☐

FEATURES

	Good	Average	Poor
Home Warranty	☐	☐	☐
Energy Saving Features	☐	☐	☐

INTERIOR

	Good	Average	Poor
Walls / Trim / Ceilings	☐	☐	☐
Flooring	☐	☐	☐
Stairs	☐	☐	☐
Storage	☐	☐	☐
Living Room	☐	☐	☐
Family Room	☐	☐	☐
Dining Room	☐	☐	☐

	Good	Average	Poor
Master Bedroom	☐	☐	☐
Bedroom 2	☐	☐	☐
Bedroom 3	☐	☐	☐
Bedroom 4	☐	☐	☐
Master Bathroom	☐	☐	☐
Bathroom 2	☐	☐	☐
Bathroom 3	☐	☐	☐
Bonus / Game Room	☐	☐	☐

	Good	Average	Poor
Kitchen	☐	☐	☐
Cabinets	☐	☐	☐
Countertop	☐	☐	☐
Counter Space	☐	☐	☐
Flooring	☐	☐	☐
Oven / Stove	☐	☐	☐
Microwave	☐	☐	☐
Layout	☐	☐	☐
Light Fixtures	☐	☐	☐
Backsplash	☐	☐	☐
Pantry	☐	☐	☐
Appliances	☐	☐	☐
Island	☐	☐	☐

	Good	Average	Poor
Basement	☐	☐	☐
Garage	☐	☐	☐

COMMUNITY

	Good	Average	Poor
Immediate Neighborhood	☐	☐	☐
Close to Employment	☐	☐	☐
Close to Shopping	☐	☐	☐
Close to Transportation	☐	☐	☐
Close to Schools / Daycare	☐	☐	☐
Close to Places of Worship	☐	☐	☐
Near Recreational Facilities	☐	☐	☐
Close to Airport	☐	☐	☐
Near Police and Fire Department	☐	☐	☐

14

Address _____ Price _____

Bedrooms _____ Bathrooms _____ Sq.Ft. _____

Lot Size: _____ Year Built _____ School District _____

Annual Tax _____

EXTERIOR

	Good	Average	Poor
View/Yard/Landscaping	☐	☐	☐
Trees	☐	☐	☐
Lawn (Front)	☐	☐	☐
Lawn (Back)	☐	☐	☐
Fences (condition)	☐	☐	☐
Landscaping (condition)	☐	☐	☐
Irrigation / Sprinkler	☐	☐	☐
	☐	☐	☐
House Type	☐	☐	☐
Exterior Siding	☐	☐	☐
Deck / Patio / Porch	☐	☐	☐
Garage	☐	☐	☐
Window / Doors	☐	☐	☐
Roof / Gutters	☐	☐	☐
Fencing	☐	☐	☐

HOME SYSTEMS

	Good	Average	Poor
Electrical	☐	☐	☐
Air Conditioning / Fans	☐	☐	☐
Heating	☐	☐	☐
Security	☐	☐	☐
Plumbing	☐	☐	☐
Intercom	☐	☐	☐

FEATURES

	Good	Average	Poor
Home Warranty	☐	☐	☐
Energy Saving Features	☐	☐	☐

INTERIOR

	Good	Average	Poor
Walls / Trim / Ceilings	☐	☐	☐
Flooring	☐	☐	☐
Stairs	☐	☐	☐
Storage	☐	☐	☐
Living Room	☐	☐	☐
Family Room	☐	☐	☐
Dining Room	☐	☐	☐

	Good	Average	Poor
Master Bedroom	☐	☐	☐
Bedroom 2	☐	☐	☐
Bedroom 3	☐	☐	☐
Bedroom 4	☐	☐	☐
Master Bathroom	☐	☐	☐
Bathroom 2	☐	☐	☐
Bathroom 3	☐	☐	☐
Bonus / Game Room	☐	☐	☐

	Good	Average	Poor
Kitchen	☐	☐	☐
Cabinets	☐	☐	☐
Countertop	☐	☐	☐
Counter Space	☐	☐	☐
Flooring	☐	☐	☐
Oven / Stove	☐	☐	☐
Microwave	☐	☐	☐
Layout	☐	☐	☐
Light Fixtures	☐	☐	☐
Backsplash	☐	☐	☐
Pantry	☐	☐	☐
Appliances	☐	☐	☐
Island	☐	☐	☐

	Good	Average	Poor
Basement	☐	☐	☐
Garage	☐	☐	☐

COMMUNITY

	Good	Average	Poor
Immediate Neighborhood	☐	☐	☐
Close to Employment	☐	☐	☐
Close to Shopping	☐	☐	☐
Close to Transportation	☐	☐	☐
Close to Schools / Daycare	☐	☐	☐
Close to Places of Worship	☐	☐	☐
Near Recreational Facilities	☐	☐	☐
Close to Airport	☐	☐	☐
Near Police and Fire Department	☐	☐	☐

Address _____   Price _____

Bedrooms _____   Bathrooms _____   Sq.Ft. _____

Lot Size: _____   Year Built _____   School District _____

Annual Tax _____

EXTERIOR

	Good	Average	Poor
View/Yard/Landscaping	☐	☐	☐
Trees	☐	☐	☐
Lawn (Front)	☐	☐	☐
Lawn (Back)	☐	☐	☐
Fences (condition)	☐	☐	☐
Landscaping (condition)	☐	☐	☐
Irrigation / Sprinkler	☐	☐	☐
	☐	☐	☐
House Type	☐	☐	☐
Exterior Siding	☐	☐	☐
Deck / Patio / Porch	☐	☐	☐
Garage	☐	☐	☐
Window / Doors	☐	☐	☐
Roof / Gutters	☐	☐	☐
Fencing	☐	☐	☐

HOME SYSTEMS

	Good	Average	Poor
Electrical	☐	☐	☐
Air Conditioning / Fans	☐	☐	☐
Heating	☐	☐	☐
Security	☐	☐	☐
Plumbing	☐	☐	☐
Intercom	☐	☐	☐

FEATURES

	Good	Average	Poor
Home Warranty	☐	☐	☐
Energy Saving Features	☐	☐	☐

INTERIOR

	Good	Average	Poor
Walls / Trim / Ceilings	☐	☐	☐
Flooring	☐	☐	☐
Stairs	☐	☐	☐
Storage	☐	☐	☐
Living Room	☐	☐	☐
Family Room	☐	☐	☐
Dining Room	☐	☐	☐

	Good	Average	Poor
Master Bedroom	☐	☐	☐
Bedroom 2	☐	☐	☐
Bedroom 3	☐	☐	☐
Bedroom 4	☐	☐	☐
Master Bathroom	☐	☐	☐
Bathroom 2	☐	☐	☐
Bathroom 3	☐	☐	☐
Bonus / Game Room	☐	☐	☐

	Good	Average	Poor
Kitchen	☐	☐	☐
Cabinets	☐	☐	☐
Countertop	☐	☐	☐
Counter Space	☐	☐	☐
Flooring	☐	☐	☐
Oven / Stove	☐	☐	☐
Microwave	☐	☐	☐
Layout	☐	☐	☐
Light Fixtures	☐	☐	☐
Backsplash	☐	☐	☐
Pantry	☐	☐	☐
Appliances	☐	☐	☐
Island	☐	☐	☐

	Good	Average	Poor
Basement	☐	☐	☐
Garage	☐	☐	☐

COMMUNITY

	Good	Average	Poor
Immediate Neighborhood	☐	☐	☐
Close to Employment	☐	☐	☐
Close to Shopping	☐	☐	☐
Close to Transportation	☐	☐	☐
Close to Schools / Daycare	☐	☐	☐
Close to Places of Worship	☐	☐	☐
Near Recreational Facilities	☐	☐	☐
Close to Airport	☐	☐	☐
Near Police and Fire Department	☐	☐	☐

Address _____   Price _____

Bedrooms _____   Bathrooms _____   Sq.Ft. _____

Lot Size: _____   Year Built _____   School District _____

Annual Tax _____

EXTERIOR

	Good	Average	Poor
View/Yard/Landscaping	☐	☐	☐
Trees	☐	☐	☐
Lawn (Front)	☐	☐	☐
Lawn (Back)	☐	☐	☐
Fences (condition)	☐	☐	☐
Landscaping (condition)	☐	☐	☐
Irrigation / Sprinkler	☐	☐	☐
	☐	☐	☐
House Type	☐	☐	☐
Exterior Siding	☐	☐	☐
Deck / Patio / Porch	☐	☐	☐
Garage	☐	☐	☐
Window / Doors	☐	☐	☐
Roof / Gutters	☐	☐	☐
Fencing	☐	☐	☐

HOME SYSTEMS

	Good	Average	Poor
Electrical	☐	☐	☐
Air Conditioning / Fans	☐	☐	☐
Heating	☐	☐	☐
Security	☐	☐	☐
Plumbing	☐	☐	☐
Intercom	☐	☐	☐

FEATURES

	Good	Average	Poor
Home Warranty	☐	☐	☐
Energy Saving Features	☐	☐	☐

INTERIOR

	Good	Average	Poor
Walls / Trim / Ceilings	☐	☐	☐
Flooring	☐	☐	☐
Stairs	☐	☐	☐
Storage	☐	☐	☐
Living Room	☐	☐	☐
Family Room	☐	☐	☐
Dining Room	☐	☐	☐

	Good	Average	Poor
Master Bedroom	☐	☐	☐
Bedroom 2	☐	☐	☐
Bedroom 3	☐	☐	☐
Bedroom 4	☐	☐	☐
Master Bathroom	☐	☐	☐
Bathroom 2	☐	☐	☐
Bathroom 3	☐	☐	☐
Bonus / Game Room	☐	☐	☐

	Good	Average	Poor
Kitchen	☐	☐	☐
Cabinets	☐	☐	☐
Countertop	☐	☐	☐
Counter Space	☐	☐	☐
Flooring	☐	☐	☐
Oven / Stove	☐	☐	☐
Microwave	☐	☐	☐
Layout	☐	☐	☐
Light Fixtures	☐	☐	☐
Backsplash	☐	☐	☐
Pantry	☐	☐	☐
Appliances	☐	☐	☐
Island	☐	☐	☐

	Good	Average	Poor
Basement	☐	☐	☐
Garage	☐	☐	☐

COMMUNITY

	Good	Average	Poor
Immediate Neighborhood	☐	☐	☐
Close to Employment	☐	☐	☐
Close to Shopping	☐	☐	☐
Close to Transportation	☐	☐	☐
Close to Schools / Daycare	☐	☐	☐
Close to Places of Worship	☐	☐	☐
Near Recreational Facilities	☐	☐	☐
Close to Airport	☐	☐	☐
Near Police and Fire Department	☐	☐	☐

Address _____   Price _____

Bedrooms _____   Bathrooms _____   Sq.Ft. _____

Lot Size: _____   Year Built _____   School District _____

Annual Tax _____

EXTERIOR

	Good	Average	Poor
View/Yard/Landscaping	☐	☐	☐
Trees	☐	☐	☐
Lawn (Front)	☐	☐	☐
Lawn (Back)	☐	☐	☐
Fences (condition)	☐	☐	☐
Landscaping (condition)	☐	☐	☐
Irrigation / Sprinkler	☐	☐	☐
	☐	☐	☐
House Type	☐	☐	☐
Exterior Siding	☐	☐	☐
Deck / Patio / Porch	☐	☐	☐
Garage	☐	☐	☐
Window / Doors	☐	☐	☐
Roof / Gutters	☐	☐	☐
Fencing	☐	☐	☐

HOME SYSTEMS

	Good	Average	Poor
Electrical	☐	☐	☐
Air Conditioning / Fans	☐	☐	☐
Heating	☐	☐	☐
Security	☐	☐	☐
Plumbing	☐	☐	☐
Intercom	☐	☐	☐

FEATURES

	Good	Average	Poor
Home Warranty	☐	☐	☐
Energy Saving Features	☐	☐	☐

INTERIOR

	Good	Average	Poor
Walls / Trim / Ceilings	☐	☐	☐
Flooring	☐	☐	☐
Stairs	☐	☐	☐
Storage	☐	☐	☐
Living Room	☐	☐	☐
Family Room	☐	☐	☐
Dining Room	☐	☐	☐

	Good	Average	Poor
Master Bedroom	☐	☐	☐
Bedroom 2	☐	☐	☐
Bedroom 3	☐	☐	☐
Bedroom 4	☐	☐	☐
Master Bathroom	☐	☐	☐
Bathroom 2	☐	☐	☐
Bathroom 3	☐	☐	☐
Bonus / Game Room	☐	☐	☐

	Good	Average	Poor
Kitchen	☐	☐	☐
Cabinets	☐	☐	☐
Countertop	☐	☐	☐
Counter Space	☐	☐	☐
Flooring	☐	☐	☐
Oven / Stove	☐	☐	☐
Microwave	☐	☐	☐
Layout	☐	☐	☐
Light Fixtures	☐	☐	☐
Backsplash	☐	☐	☐
Pantry	☐	☐	☐
Appliances	☐	☐	☐
Island	☐	☐	☐

	Good	Average	Poor
Basement	☐	☐	☐
Garage	☐	☐	☐

COMMUNITY

	Good	Average	Poor
Immediate Neighborhood	☐	☐	☐
Close to Employment	☐	☐	☐
Close to Shopping	☐	☐	☐
Close to Transportation	☐	☐	☐
Close to Schools / Daycare	☐	☐	☐
Close to Places of Worship	☐	☐	☐
Near Recreational Facilities	☐	☐	☐
Close to Airport	☐	☐	☐
Near Police and Fire Department	☐	☐	☐

Address _____   Price _____

Bedrooms _____   Bathrooms _____   Sq.Ft. _____

Lot Size: _____   Year Built _____   School District _____

Annual Tax _____

EXTERIOR

	Good	Average	Poor
View/Yard/Landscaping	☐	☐	☐
Trees	☐	☐	☐
Lawn (Front)	☐	☐	☐
Lawn (Back)	☐	☐	☐
Fences (condition)	☐	☐	☐
Landscaping (condition)	☐	☐	☐
Irrigation / Sprinkler	☐	☐	☐
	☐	☐	☐
House Type	☐	☐	☐
Exterior Siding	☐	☐	☐
Deck / Patio / Porch	☐	☐	☐
Garage	☐	☐	☐
Window / Doors	☐	☐	☐
Roof / Gutters	☐	☐	☐
Fencing	☐	☐	☐

HOME SYSTEMS

	Good	Average	Poor
Electrical	☐	☐	☐
Air Conditioning / Fans	☐	☐	☐
Heating	☐	☐	☐
Security	☐	☐	☐
Plumbing	☐	☐	☐
Intercom	☐	☐	☐

FEATURES

	Good	Average	Poor
Home Warranty	☐	☐	☐
Energy Saving Features	☐	☐	☐

INTERIOR

	Good	Average	Poor
Walls / Trim / Ceilings	☐	☐	☐
Flooring	☐	☐	☐
Stairs	☐	☐	☐
Storage	☐	☐	☐
Living Room	☐	☐	☐
Family Room	☐	☐	☐
Dining Room	☐	☐	☐

	Good	Average	Poor
Master Bedroom	☐	☐	☐
Bedroom 2	☐	☐	☐
Bedroom 3	☐	☐	☐
Bedroom 4	☐	☐	☐
Master Bathroom	☐	☐	☐
Bathroom 2	☐	☐	☐
Bathroom 3	☐	☐	☐
Bonus / Game Room	☐	☐	☐

	Good	Average	Poor
Kitchen	☐	☐	☐
Cabinets	☐	☐	☐
Countertop	☐	☐	☐
Counter Space	☐	☐	☐
Flooring	☐	☐	☐
Oven / Stove	☐	☐	☐
Microwave	☐	☐	☐
Layout	☐	☐	☐
Light Fixtures	☐	☐	☐
Backsplash	☐	☐	☐
Pantry	☐	☐	☐
Appliances	☐	☐	☐
Island	☐	☐	☐

	Good	Average	Poor
Basement	☐	☐	☐
Garage	☐	☐	☐

COMMUNITY

	Good	Average	Poor
Immediate Neighborhood	☐	☐	☐
Close to Employment	☐	☐	☐
Close to Shopping	☐	☐	☐
Close to Transportation	☐	☐	☐
Close to Schools / Daycare	☐	☐	☐
Close to Places of Worship	☐	☐	☐
Near Recreational Facilities	☐	☐	☐
Close to Airport	☐	☐	☐
Near Police and Fire Department	☐	☐	☐

19

Address _____ Price _____

Bedrooms _____ Bathrooms _____ Sq.Ft. _____

Lot Size: _____ Year Built _____ School District _____

Annual Tax _____

EXTERIOR

	Good	Average	Poor
View/Yard/Landscaping	☐	☐	☐
Trees	☐	☐	☐
Lawn (Front)	☐	☐	☐
Lawn (Back)	☐	☐	☐
Fences (condition)	☐	☐	☐
Landscaping (condition)	☐	☐	☐
Irrigation / Sprinkler	☐	☐	☐
	☐	☐	☐
House Type	☐	☐	☐
Exterior Siding	☐	☐	☐
Deck / Patio / Porch	☐	☐	☐
Garage	☐	☐	☐
Window / Doors	☐	☐	☐
Roof / Gutters	☐	☐	☐
Fencing	☐	☐	☐

HOME SYSTEMS

	Good	Average	Poor
Electrical	☐	☐	☐
Air Conditioning / Fans	☐	☐	☐
Heating	☐	☐	☐
Security	☐	☐	☐
Plumbing	☐	☐	☐
Intercom	☐	☐	☐

FEATURES

	Good	Average	Poor
Home Warranty	☐	☐	☐
Energy Saving Features	☐	☐	☐

INTERIOR

	Good	Average	Poor
Walls / Trim / Ceilings	☐	☐	☐
Flooring	☐	☐	☐
Stairs	☐	☐	☐
Storage	☐	☐	☐
Living Room	☐	☐	☐
Family Room	☐	☐	☐
Dining Room	☐	☐	☐

	Good	Average	Poor
Master Bedroom	☐	☐	☐
Bedroom 2	☐	☐	☐
Bedroom 3	☐	☐	☐
Bedroom 4	☐	☐	☐
Master Bathroom	☐	☐	☐
Bathroom 2	☐	☐	☐
Bathroom 3	☐	☐	☐
Bonus / Game Room	☐	☐	☐

	Good	Average	Poor
Kitchen	☐	☐	☐
Cabinets	☐	☐	☐
Countertop	☐	☐	☐
Counter Space	☐	☐	☐
Flooring	☐	☐	☐
Oven / Stove	☐	☐	☐
Microwave	☐	☐	☐
Layout	☐	☐	☐
Light Fixtures	☐	☐	☐
Backsplash	☐	☐	☐
Pantry	☐	☐	☐
Appliances	☐	☐	☐
Island	☐	☐	☐

	Good	Average	Poor
Basement	☐	☐	☐
Garage	☐	☐	☐

COMMUNITY

	Good	Average	Poor
Immediate Neighborhood	☐	☐	☐
Close to Employment	☐	☐	☐
Close to Shopping	☐	☐	☐
Close to Transportation	☐	☐	☐
Close to Schools / Daycare	☐	☐	☐
Close to Places of Worship	☐	☐	☐
Near Recreational Facilities	☐	☐	☐
Close to Airport	☐	☐	☐
Near Police and Fire Department	☐	☐	☐

20

Address _____   Price _____

Bedrooms _____   Bathrooms _____   Sq.Ft. _____

Lot Size: _____   Year Built _____   School District _____

Annual Tax _____

EXTERIOR

	Good	Average	Poor
View/Yard/Landscaping	☐	☐	☐
Trees	☐	☐	☐
Lawn (Front)	☐	☐	☐
Lawn (Back)	☐	☐	☐
Fences (condition)	☐	☐	☐
Landscaping (condition)	☐	☐	☐
Irrigation / Sprinkler	☐	☐	☐
	☐	☐	☐
House Type	☐	☐	☐
Exterior Siding	☐	☐	☐
Deck / Patio / Porch	☐	☐	☐
Garage	☐	☐	☐
Window / Doors	☐	☐	☐
Roof / Gutters	☐	☐	☐
Fencing	☐	☐	☐

HOME SYSTEMS

	Good	Average	Poor
Electrical	☐	☐	☐
Air Conditioning / Fans	☐	☐	☐
Heating	☐	☐	☐
Security	☐	☐	☐
Plumbing	☐	☐	☐
Intercom	☐	☐	☐

FEATURES

	Good	Average	Poor
Home Warranty	☐	☐	☐
Energy Saving Features	☐	☐	☐

INTERIOR

	Good	Average	Poor
Walls / Trim / Ceilings	☐	☐	☐
Flooring	☐	☐	☐
Stairs	☐	☐	☐
Storage	☐	☐	☐
Living Room	☐	☐	☐
Family Room	☐	☐	☐
Dining Room	☐	☐	☐

	Good	Average	Poor
Master Bedroom	☐	☐	☐
Bedroom 2	☐	☐	☐
Bedroom 3	☐	☐	☐
Bedroom 4	☐	☐	☐
Master Bathroom	☐	☐	☐
Bathroom 2	☐	☐	☐
Bathroom 3	☐	☐	☐
Bonus / Game Room	☐	☐	☐

	Good	Average	Poor
Kitchen	☐	☐	☐
Cabinets	☐	☐	☐
Countertop	☐	☐	☐
Counter Space	☐	☐	☐
Flooring	☐	☐	☐
Oven / Stove	☐	☐	☐
Microwave	☐	☐	☐
Layout	☐	☐	☐
Light Fixtures	☐	☐	☐
Backsplash	☐	☐	☐
Pantry	☐	☐	☐
Appliances	☐	☐	☐
Island	☐	☐	☐

	Good	Average	Poor
Basement	☐	☐	☐
Garage	☐	☐	☐

COMMUNITY

	Good	Average	Poor
Immediate Neighborhood	☐	☐	☐
Close to Employment	☐	☐	☐
Close to Shopping	☐	☐	☐
Close to Transportation	☐	☐	☐
Close to Schools / Daycare	☐	☐	☐
Close to Places of Worship	☐	☐	☐
Near Recreational Facilities	☐	☐	☐
Close to Airport	☐	☐	☐
Near Police and Fire Department	☐	☐	☐

Address _____   Price _____

Bedrooms _____   Bathrooms _____   Sq.Ft. _____

Lot Size: _____   Year Built _____   School District _____

Annual Tax _____

EXTERIOR

	Good	Average	Poor
View/Yard/Landscaping	☐	☐	☐
Trees	☐	☐	☐
Lawn (Front)	☐	☐	☐
Lawn (Back)	☐	☐	☐
Fences (condition)	☐	☐	☐
Landscaping (condition)	☐	☐	☐
Irrigation / Sprinkler	☐	☐	☐
	☐	☐	☐
House Type	☐	☐	☐
Exterior Siding	☐	☐	☐
Deck / Patio / Porch	☐	☐	☐
Garage	☐	☐	☐
Window / Doors	☐	☐	☐
Roof / Gutters	☐	☐	☐
Fencing	☐	☐	☐

HOME SYSTEMS

	Good	Average	Poor
Electrical	☐	☐	☐
Air Conditioning / Fans	☐	☐	☐
Heating	☐	☐	☐
Security	☐	☐	☐
Plumbing	☐	☐	☐
Intercom	☐	☐	☐

FEATURES

	Good	Average	Poor
Home Warranty	☐	☐	☐
Energy Saving Features	☐	☐	☐

INTERIOR

	Good	Average	Poor
Walls / Trim / Ceilings	☐	☐	☐
Flooring	☐	☐	☐
Stairs	☐	☐	☐
Storage	☐	☐	☐
Living Room	☐	☐	☐
Family Room	☐	☐	☐
Dining Room	☐	☐	☐

	Good	Average	Poor
Master Bedroom	☐	☐	☐
Bedroom 2	☐	☐	☐
Bedroom 3	☐	☐	☐
Bedroom 4	☐	☐	☐
Master Bathroom	☐	☐	☐
Bathroom 2	☐	☐	☐
Bathroom 3	☐	☐	☐
Bonus / Game Room	☐	☐	☐

	Good	Average	Poor
Kitchen	☐	☐	☐
Cabinets	☐	☐	☐
Countertop	☐	☐	☐
Counter Space	☐	☐	☐
Flooring	☐	☐	☐
Oven / Stove	☐	☐	☐
Microwave	☐	☐	☐
Layout	☐	☐	☐
Light Fixtures	☐	☐	☐
Backsplash	☐	☐	☐
Pantry	☐	☐	☐
Appliances	☐	☐	☐
Island	☐	☐	☐

	Good	Average	Poor
Basement	☐	☐	☐
Garage	☐	☐	☐

COMMUNITY

	Good	Average	Poor
Immediate Neighborhood	☐	☐	☐
Close to Employment	☐	☐	☐
Close to Shopping	☐	☐	☐
Close to Transportation	☐	☐	☐
Close to Schools / Daycare	☐	☐	☐
Close to Places of Worship	☐	☐	☐
Near Recreational Facilities	☐	☐	☐
Close to Airport	☐	☐	☐
Near Police and Fire Department	☐	☐	☐

Address _____ Price _____

Bedrooms _____ Bathrooms _____ Sq.Ft. _____

Lot Size: _____ Year Built _____ School District _____

Annual Tax _____

EXTERIOR

	Good	Average	Poor
View/Yard/Landscaping	☐	☐	☐
Trees	☐	☐	☐
Lawn (Front)	☐	☐	☐
Lawn (Back)	☐	☐	☐
Fences (condition)	☐	☐	☐
Landscaping (condition)	☐	☐	☐
Irrigation / Sprinkler	☐	☐	☐
	☐	☐	☐
House Type	☐	☐	☐
Exterior Siding	☐	☐	☐
Deck / Patio / Porch	☐	☐	☐
Garage	☐	☐	☐
Window / Doors	☐	☐	☐
Roof / Gutters	☐	☐	☐
Fencing	☐	☐	☐

HOME SYSTEMS

	Good	Average	Poor
Electrical	☐	☐	☐
Air Conditioning / Fans	☐	☐	☐
Heating	☐	☐	☐
Security	☐	☐	☐
Plumbing	☐	☐	☐
Intercom	☐	☐	☐

FEATURES

	Good	Average	Poor
Home Warranty	☐	☐	☐
Energy Saving Features	☐	☐	☐

INTERIOR

	Good	Average	Poor
Walls / Trim / Ceilings	☐	☐	☐
Flooring	☐	☐	☐
Stairs	☐	☐	☐
Storage	☐	☐	☐
Living Room	☐	☐	☐
Family Room	☐	☐	☐
Dining Room	☐	☐	☐

	Good	Average	Poor
Master Bedroom	☐	☐	☐
Bedroom 2	☐	☐	☐
Bedroom 3	☐	☐	☐
Bedroom 4	☐	☐	☐
Master Bathroom	☐	☐	☐
Bathroom 2	☐	☐	☐
Bathroom 3	☐	☐	☐
Bonus / Game Room	☐	☐	☐

	Good	Average	Poor
Kitchen	☐	☐	☐
Cabinets	☐	☐	☐
Countertop	☐	☐	☐
Counter Space	☐	☐	☐
Flooring	☐	☐	☐
Oven / Stove	☐	☐	☐
Microwave	☐	☐	☐
Layout	☐	☐	☐
Light Fixtures	☐	☐	☐
Backsplash	☐	☐	☐
Pantry	☐	☐	☐
Appliances	☐	☐	☐
Island	☐	☐	☐

	Good	Average	Poor
Basement	☐	☐	☐
Garage	☐	☐	☐

COMMUNITY

	Good	Average	Poor
Immediate Neighborhood	☐	☐	☐
Close to Employment	☐	☐	☐
Close to Shopping	☐	☐	☐
Close to Transportation	☐	☐	☐
Close to Schools / Daycare	☐	☐	☐
Close to Places of Worship	☐	☐	☐
Near Recreational Facilities	☐	☐	☐
Close to Airport	☐	☐	☐
Near Police and Fire Department	☐	☐	☐

Address _____   Price _____

Bedrooms _____   Bathrooms _____   Sq.Ft. _____

Lot Size: _____   Year Built _____   School District _____

Annual Tax _____

EXTERIOR

	Good	Average	Poor
View/Yard/Landscaping	☐	☐	☐
Trees	☐	☐	☐
Lawn (Front)	☐	☐	☐
Lawn (Back)	☐	☐	☐
Fences (condition)	☐	☐	☐
Landscaping (condition)	☐	☐	☐
Irrigation / Sprinkler	☐	☐	☐
	☐	☐	☐
House Type	☐	☐	☐
Exterior Siding	☐	☐	☐
Deck / Patio / Porch	☐	☐	☐
Garage	☐	☐	☐
Window / Doors	☐	☐	☐
Roof / Gutters	☐	☐	☐
Fencing	☐	☐	☐

HOME SYSTEMS

	Good	Average	Poor
Electrical	☐	☐	☐
Air Conditioning / Fans	☐	☐	☐
Heating	☐	☐	☐
Security	☐	☐	☐
Plumbing	☐	☐	☐
Intercom	☐	☐	☐

FEATURES

	Good	Average	Poor
Home Warranty	☐	☐	☐
Energy Saving Features	☐	☐	☐

INTERIOR

	Good	Average	Poor
Walls / Trim / Ceilings	☐	☐	☐
Flooring	☐	☐	☐
Stairs	☐	☐	☐
Storage	☐	☐	☐
Living Room	☐	☐	☐
Family Room	☐	☐	☐
Dining Room	☐	☐	☐

	Good	Average	Poor
Master Bedroom	☐	☐	☐
Bedroom 2	☐	☐	☐
Bedroom 3	☐	☐	☐
Bedroom 4	☐	☐	☐
Master Bathroom	☐	☐	☐
Bathroom 2	☐	☐	☐
Bathroom 3	☐	☐	☐
Bonus / Game Room	☐	☐	☐

	Good	Average	Poor
Kitchen	☐	☐	☐
Cabinets	☐	☐	☐
Countertop	☐	☐	☐
Counter Space	☐	☐	☐
Flooring	☐	☐	☐
Oven / Stove	☐	☐	☐
Microwave	☐	☐	☐
Layout	☐	☐	☐
Light Fixtures	☐	☐	☐
Backsplash	☐	☐	☐
Pantry	☐	☐	☐
Appliances	☐	☐	☐
Island	☐	☐	☐

	Good	Average	Poor
Basement	☐	☐	☐
Garage	☐	☐	☐

COMMUNITY

	Good	Average	Poor
Immediate Neighborhood	☐	☐	☐
Close to Employment	☐	☐	☐
Close to Shopping	☐	☐	☐
Close to Transportation	☐	☐	☐
Close to Schools / Daycare	☐	☐	☐
Close to Places of Worship	☐	☐	☐
Near Recreational Facilities	☐	☐	☐
Close to Airport	☐	☐	☐
Near Police and Fire Department	☐	☐	☐

Address _____   Price _____

Bedrooms _____   Bathrooms _____   Sq.Ft. _____

Lot Size: _____   Year Built _____   School District _____

Annual Tax _____

EXTERIOR

	Good	Average	Poor
View/Yard/Landscaping	☐	☐	☐
Trees	☐	☐	☐
Lawn (Front)	☐	☐	☐
Lawn (Back)	☐	☐	☐
Fences (condition)	☐	☐	☐
Landscaping (condition)	☐	☐	☐
Irrigation / Sprinkler	☐	☐	☐
	☐	☐	☐
House Type	☐	☐	☐
Exterior Siding	☐	☐	☐
Deck / Patio / Porch	☐	☐	☐
Garage	☐	☐	☐
Window / Doors	☐	☐	☐
Roof / Gutters	☐	☐	☐
Fencing	☐	☐	☐

HOME SYSTEMS

	Good	Average	Poor
Electrical	☐	☐	☐
Air Conditioning / Fans	☐	☐	☐
Heating	☐	☐	☐
Security	☐	☐	☐
Plumbing	☐	☐	☐
Intercom	☐	☐	☐

FEATURES

	Good	Average	Poor
Home Warranty	☐	☐	☐
Energy Saving Features	☐	☐	☐

INTERIOR

	Good	Average	Poor
Walls / Trim / Ceilings	☐	☐	☐
Flooring	☐	☐	☐
Stairs	☐	☐	☐
Storage	☐	☐	☐
Living Room	☐	☐	☐
Family Room	☐	☐	☐
Dining Room	☐	☐	☐

	Good	Average	Poor
Master Bedroom	☐	☐	☐
Bedroom 2	☐	☐	☐
Bedroom 3	☐	☐	☐
Bedroom 4	☐	☐	☐
Master Bathroom	☐	☐	☐
Bathroom 2	☐	☐	☐
Bathroom 3	☐	☐	☐
Bonus / Game Room	☐	☐	☐

	Good	Average	Poor
Kitchen	☐	☐	☐
Cabinets	☐	☐	☐
Countertop	☐	☐	☐
Counter Space	☐	☐	☐
Flooring	☐	☐	☐
Oven / Stove	☐	☐	☐
Microwave	☐	☐	☐
Layout	☐	☐	☐
Light Fixtures	☐	☐	☐
Backsplash	☐	☐	☐
Pantry	☐	☐	☐
Appliances	☐	☐	☐
Island	☐	☐	☐

	Good	Average	Poor
Basement	☐	☐	☐
Garage	☐	☐	☐

COMMUNITY

	Good	Average	Poor
Immediate Neighborhood	☐	☐	☐
Close to Employment	☐	☐	☐
Close to Shopping	☐	☐	☐
Close to Transportation	☐	☐	☐
Close to Schools / Daycare	☐	☐	☐
Close to Places of Worship	☐	☐	☐
Near Recreational Facilities	☐	☐	☐
Close to Airport	☐	☐	☐
Near Police and Fire Department	☐	☐	☐

Address _____   Price _____

Bedrooms _____ Bathrooms _____ Sq.Ft. _____

Lot Size: _____ Year Built _____ School District _____

Annual Tax _____

EXTERIOR

	Good	Average	Poor
View/Yard/Landscaping	☐	☐	☐
Trees	☐	☐	☐
Lawn (Front)	☐	☐	☐
Lawn (Back)	☐	☐	☐
Fences (condition)	☐	☐	☐
Landscaping (condition)	☐	☐	☐
Irrigation / Sprinkler	☐	☐	☐
	☐	☐	☐
House Type	☐	☐	☐
Exterior Siding	☐	☐	☐
Deck / Patio / Porch	☐	☐	☐
Garage	☐	☐	☐
Window / Doors	☐	☐	☐
Roof / Gutters	☐	☐	☐
Fencing	☐	☐	☐

HOME SYSTEMS

	Good	Average	Poor
Electrical	☐	☐	☐
Air Conditioning / Fans	☐	☐	☐
Heating	☐	☐	☐
Security	☐	☐	☐
Plumbing	☐	☐	☐
Intercom	☐	☐	☐

FEATURES

	Good	Average	Poor
Home Warranty	☐	☐	☐
Energy Saving Features	☐	☐	☐

INTERIOR

	Good	Average	Poor
Walls / Trim / Ceilings	☐	☐	☐
Flooring	☐	☐	☐
Stairs	☐	☐	☐
Storage	☐	☐	☐
Living Room	☐	☐	☐
Family Room	☐	☐	☐
Dining Room	☐	☐	☐

	Good	Average	Poor
Master Bedroom	☐	☐	☐
Bedroom 2	☐	☐	☐
Bedroom 3	☐	☐	☐
Bedroom 4	☐	☐	☐
Master Bathroom	☐	☐	☐
Bathroom 2	☐	☐	☐
Bathroom 3	☐	☐	☐
Bonus / Game Room	☐	☐	☐

	Good	Average	Poor
Kitchen	☐	☐	☐
Cabinets	☐	☐	☐
Countertop	☐	☐	☐
Counter Space	☐	☐	☐
Flooring	☐	☐	☐
Oven / Stove	☐	☐	☐
Microwave	☐	☐	☐
Layout	☐	☐	☐
Light Fixtures	☐	☐	☐
Backsplash	☐	☐	☐
Pantry	☐	☐	☐
Appliances	☐	☐	☐
Island	☐	☐	☐

	Good	Average	Poor
Basement	☐	☐	☐
Garage	☐	☐	☐

COMMUNITY

	Good	Average	Poor
Immediate Neighborhood	☐	☐	☐
Close to Employment	☐	☐	☐
Close to Shopping	☐	☐	☐
Close to Transportation	☐	☐	☐
Close to Schools / Daycare	☐	☐	☐
Close to Places of Worship	☐	☐	☐
Near Recreational Facilities	☐	☐	☐
Close to Airport	☐	☐	☐
Near Police and Fire Department	☐	☐	☐

Address _____   Price _____

Bedrooms _____   Bathrooms _____   Sq.Ft. _____

Lot Size: _____   Year Built _____   School District _____

Annual Tax _____

EXTERIOR

	Good	Average	Poor
View/Yard/Landscaping	☐	☐	☐
Trees	☐	☐	☐
Lawn (Front)	☐	☐	☐
Lawn (Back)	☐	☐	☐
Fences (condition)	☐	☐	☐
Landscaping (condition)	☐	☐	☐
Irrigation / Sprinkler	☐	☐	☐
	☐	☐	☐
House Type	☐	☐	☐
Exterior Siding	☐	☐	☐
Deck / Patio / Porch	☐	☐	☐
Garage	☐	☐	☐
Window / Doors	☐	☐	☐
Roof / Gutters	☐	☐	☐
Fencing	☐	☐	☐

HOME SYSTEMS

	Good	Average	Poor
Electrical	☐	☐	☐
Air Conditioning / Fans	☐	☐	☐
Heating	☐	☐	☐
Security	☐	☐	☐
Plumbing	☐	☐	☐
Intercom	☐	☐	☐

FEATURES

	Good	Average	Poor
Home Warranty	☐	☐	☐
Energy Saving Features	☐	☐	☐

INTERIOR

	Good	Average	Poor
Walls / Trim / Ceilings	☐	☐	☐
Flooring	☐	☐	☐
Stairs	☐	☐	☐
Storage	☐	☐	☐
Living Room	☐	☐	☐
Family Room	☐	☐	☐
Dining Room	☐	☐	☐

	Good	Average	Poor
Master Bedroom	☐	☐	☐
Bedroom 2	☐	☐	☐
Bedroom 3	☐	☐	☐
Bedroom 4	☐	☐	☐
Master Bathroom	☐	☐	☐
Bathroom 2	☐	☐	☐
Bathroom 3	☐	☐	☐
Bonus / Game Room	☐	☐	☐

	Good	Average	Poor
Kitchen	☐	☐	☐
Cabinets	☐	☐	☐
Countertop	☐	☐	☐
Counter Space	☐	☐	☐
Flooring	☐	☐	☐
Oven / Stove	☐	☐	☐
Microwave	☐	☐	☐
Layout	☐	☐	☐
Light Fixtures	☐	☐	☐
Backsplash	☐	☐	☐
Pantry	☐	☐	☐
Appliances	☐	☐	☐
Island	☐	☐	☐

	Good	Average	Poor
Basement	☐	☐	☐
Garage	☐	☐	☐

COMMUNITY

	Good	Average	Poor
Immediate Neighborhood	☐	☐	☐
Close to Employment	☐	☐	☐
Close to Shopping	☐	☐	☐
Close to Transportation	☐	☐	☐
Close to Schools / Daycare	☐	☐	☐
Close to Places of Worship	☐	☐	☐
Near Recreational Facilities	☐	☐	☐
Close to Airport	☐	☐	☐
Near Police and Fire Department	☐	☐	☐

27

Address _____   Price _____

Bedrooms _____   Bathrooms _____   Sq.Ft. _____

Lot Size: _____   Year Built _____   School District _____

Annual Tax _____

EXTERIOR

	Good	Average	Poor
View/Yard/Landscaping	☐	☐	☐
Trees	☐	☐	☐
Lawn (Front)	☐	☐	☐
Lawn (Back)	☐	☐	☐
Fences (condition)	☐	☐	☐
Landscaping (condition)	☐	☐	☐
Irrigation / Sprinkler	☐	☐	☐
	☐	☐	☐
House Type	☐	☐	☐
Exterior Siding	☐	☐	☐
Deck / Patio / Porch	☐	☐	☐
Garage	☐	☐	☐
Window / Doors	☐	☐	☐
Roof / Gutters	☐	☐	☐
Fencing	☐	☐	☐

HOME SYSTEMS

	Good	Average	Poor
Electrical	☐	☐	☐
Air Conditioning / Fans	☐	☐	☐
Heating	☐	☐	☐
Security	☐	☐	☐
Plumbing	☐	☐	☐
Intercom	☐	☐	☐

FEATURES

	Good	Average	Poor
Home Warranty	☐	☐	☐
Energy Saving Features	☐	☐	☐

INTERIOR

	Good	Average	Poor
Walls / Trim / Ceilings	☐	☐	☐
Flooring	☐	☐	☐
Stairs	☐	☐	☐
Storage	☐	☐	☐
Living Room	☐	☐	☐
Family Room	☐	☐	☐
Dining Room	☐	☐	☐

	Good	Average	Poor
Master Bedroom	☐	☐	☐
Bedroom 2	☐	☐	☐
Bedroom 3	☐	☐	☐
Bedroom 4	☐	☐	☐
Master Bathroom	☐	☐	☐
Bathroom 2	☐	☐	☐
Bathroom 3	☐	☐	☐
Bonus / Game Room	☐	☐	☐

	Good	Average	Poor
Kitchen	☐	☐	☐
Cabinets	☐	☐	☐
Countertop	☐	☐	☐
Counter Space	☐	☐	☐
Flooring	☐	☐	☐
Oven / Stove	☐	☐	☐
Microwave	☐	☐	☐
Layout	☐	☐	☐
Light Fixtures	☐	☐	☐
Backsplash	☐	☐	☐
Pantry	☐	☐	☐
Appliances	☐	☐	☐
Island	☐	☐	☐

	Good	Average	Poor
Basement	☐	☐	☐
Garage	☐	☐	☐

COMMUNITY

	Good	Average	Poor
Immediate Neighborhood	☐	☐	☐
Close to Employment	☐	☐	☐
Close to Shopping	☐	☐	☐
Close to Transportation	☐	☐	☐
Close to Schools / Daycare	☐	☐	☐
Close to Places of Worship	☐	☐	☐
Near Recreational Facilities	☐	☐	☐
Close to Airport	☐	☐	☐
Near Police and Fire Department	☐	☐	☐

Address _____   Price _____

Bedrooms _____ Bathrooms _____ Sq.Ft. _____

Lot Size: _____ Year Built _____ School District _____

Annual Tax _____

EXTERIOR

	Good	Average	Poor
View/Yard/Landscaping	☐	☐	☐
Trees	☐	☐	☐
Lawn (Front)	☐	☐	☐
Lawn (Back)	☐	☐	☐
Fences (condition)	☐	☐	☐
Landscaping (condition)	☐	☐	☐
Irrigation / Sprinkler	☐	☐	☐
	☐	☐	☐
House Type	☐	☐	☐
Exterior Siding	☐	☐	☐
Deck / Patio / Porch	☐	☐	☐
Garage	☐	☐	☐
Window / Doors	☐	☐	☐
Roof / Gutters	☐	☐	☐
Fencing	☐	☐	☐

HOME SYSTEMS

	Good	Average	Poor
Electrical	☐	☐	☐
Air Conditioning / Fans	☐	☐	☐
Heating	☐	☐	☐
Security	☐	☐	☐
Plumbing	☐	☐	☐
Intercom	☐	☐	☐

FEATURES

	Good	Average	Poor
Home Warranty	☐	☐	☐
Energy Saving Features	☐	☐	☐

INTERIOR

	Good	Average	Poor
Walls / Trim / Ceilings	☐	☐	☐
Flooring	☐	☐	☐
Stairs	☐	☐	☐
Storage	☐	☐	☐
Living Room	☐	☐	☐
Family Room	☐	☐	☐
Dining Room	☐	☐	☐

	Good	Average	Poor
Master Bedroom	☐	☐	☐
Bedroom 2	☐	☐	☐
Bedroom 3	☐	☐	☐
Bedroom 4	☐	☐	☐
Master Bathroom	☐	☐	☐
Bathroom 2	☐	☐	☐
Bathroom 3	☐	☐	☐
Bonus / Game Room	☐	☐	☐

	Good	Average	Poor
Kitchen	☐	☐	☐
Cabinets	☐	☐	☐
Countertop	☐	☐	☐
Counter Space	☐	☐	☐
Flooring	☐	☐	☐
Oven / Stove	☐	☐	☐
Microwave	☐	☐	☐
Layout	☐	☐	☐
Light Fixtures	☐	☐	☐
Backsplash	☐	☐	☐
Pantry	☐	☐	☐
Appliances	☐	☐	☐
Island	☐	☐	☐

	Good	Average	Poor
Basement	☐	☐	☐
Garage	☐	☐	☐

COMMUNITY

	Good	Average	Poor
Immediate Neighborhood	☐	☐	☐
Close to Employment	☐	☐	☐
Close to Shopping	☐	☐	☐
Close to Transportation	☐	☐	☐
Close to Schools / Daycare	☐	☐	☐
Close to Places of Worship	☐	☐	☐
Near Recreational Facilities	☐	☐	☐
Close to Airport	☐	☐	☐
Near Police and Fire Department	☐	☐	☐

Address _____ Price _____

Bedrooms _____ Bathrooms _____ Sq.Ft. _____

Lot Size: _____ Year Built _____ School District _____

Annual Tax _____

EXTERIOR

	Good	Average	Poor
View/Yard/Landscaping	☐	☐	☐
Trees	☐	☐	☐
Lawn (Front)	☐	☐	☐
Lawn (Back)	☐	☐	☐
Fences (condition)	☐	☐	☐
Landscaping (condition)	☐	☐	☐
Irrigation / Sprinkler	☐	☐	☐
	☐	☐	☐
House Type	☐	☐	☐
Exterior Siding	☐	☐	☐
Deck / Patio / Porch	☐	☐	☐
Garage	☐	☐	☐
Window / Doors	☐	☐	☐
Roof / Gutters	☐	☐	☐
Fencing	☐	☐	☐

HOME SYSTEMS

	Good	Average	Poor
Electrical	☐	☐	☐
Air Conditioning / Fans	☐	☐	☐
Heating	☐	☐	☐
Security	☐	☐	☐
Plumbing	☐	☐	☐
Intercom	☐	☐	☐

FEATURES

	Good	Average	Poor
Home Warranty	☐	☐	☐
Energy Saving Features	☐	☐	☐

INTERIOR

	Good	Average	Poor
Walls / Trim / Ceilings	☐	☐	☐
Flooring	☐	☐	☐
Stairs	☐	☐	☐
Storage	☐	☐	☐
Living Room	☐	☐	☐
Family Room	☐	☐	☐
Dining Room	☐	☐	☐

	Good	Average	Poor
Master Bedroom	☐	☐	☐
Bedroom 2	☐	☐	☐
Bedroom 3	☐	☐	☐
Bedroom 4	☐	☐	☐
Master Bathroom	☐	☐	☐
Bathroom 2	☐	☐	☐
Bathroom 3	☐	☐	☐
Bonus / Game Room	☐	☐	☐

	Good	Average	Poor
Kitchen	☐	☐	☐
Cabinets	☐	☐	☐
Countertop	☐	☐	☐
Counter Space	☐	☐	☐
Flooring	☐	☐	☐
Oven / Stove	☐	☐	☐
Microwave	☐	☐	☐
Layout	☐	☐	☐
Light Fixtures	☐	☐	☐
Backsplash	☐	☐	☐
Pantry	☐	☐	☐
Appliances	☐	☐	☐
Island	☐	☐	☐

	Good	Average	Poor
Basement	☐	☐	☐
Garage	☐	☐	☐

COMMUNITY

	Good	Average	Poor
Immediate Neighborhood	☐	☐	☐
Close to Employment	☐	☐	☐
Close to Shopping	☐	☐	☐
Close to Transportation	☐	☐	☐
Close to Schools / Daycare	☐	☐	☐
Close to Places of Worship	☐	☐	☐
Near Recreational Facilities	☐	☐	☐
Close to Airport	☐	☐	☐
Near Police and Fire Department	☐	☐	☐

Address _____   Price _____

Bedrooms _____   Bathrooms _____   Sq.Ft. _____

Lot Size: _____   Year Built _____   School District _____

Annual Tax _____

EXTERIOR

	Good	Average	Poor
View/Yard/Landscaping	☐	☐	☐
Trees	☐	☐	☐
Lawn (Front)	☐	☐	☐
Lawn (Back)	☐	☐	☐
Fences (condition)	☐	☐	☐
Landscaping (condition)	☐	☐	☐
Irrigation / Sprinkler	☐	☐	☐
	☐	☐	☐
House Type	☐	☐	☐
Exterior Siding	☐	☐	☐
Deck / Patio / Porch	☐	☐	☐
Garage	☐	☐	☐
Window / Doors	☐	☐	☐
Roof / Gutters	☐	☐	☐
Fencing	☐	☐	☐

HOME SYSTEMS

	Good	Average	Poor
Electrical	☐	☐	☐
Air Conditioning / Fans	☐	☐	☐
Heating	☐	☐	☐
Security	☐	☐	☐
Plumbing	☐	☐	☐
Intercom	☐	☐	☐

FEATURES

	Good	Average	Poor
Home Warranty	☐	☐	☐
Energy Saving Features	☐	☐	☐

INTERIOR

	Good	Average	Poor
Walls / Trim / Ceilings	☐	☐	☐
Flooring	☐	☐	☐
Stairs	☐	☐	☐
Storage	☐	☐	☐
Living Room	☐	☐	☐
Family Room	☐	☐	☐
Dining Room	☐	☐	☐

	Good	Average	Poor
Master Bedroom	☐	☐	☐
Bedroom 2	☐	☐	☐
Bedroom 3	☐	☐	☐
Bedroom 4	☐	☐	☐
Master Bathroom	☐	☐	☐
Bathroom 2	☐	☐	☐
Bathroom 3	☐	☐	☐
Bonus / Game Room	☐	☐	☐

	Good	Average	Poor
Kitchen	☐	☐	☐
Cabinets	☐	☐	☐
Countertop	☐	☐	☐
Counter Space	☐	☐	☐
Flooring	☐	☐	☐
Oven / Stove	☐	☐	☐
Microwave	☐	☐	☐
Layout	☐	☐	☐
Light Fixtures	☐	☐	☐
Backsplash	☐	☐	☐
Pantry	☐	☐	☐
Appliances	☐	☐	☐
Island	☐	☐	☐

	Good	Average	Poor
Basement	☐	☐	☐
Garage	☐	☐	☐

COMMUNITY

	Good	Average	Poor
Immediate Neighborhood	☐	☐	☐
Close to Employment	☐	☐	☐
Close to Shopping	☐	☐	☐
Close to Transportation	☐	☐	☐
Close to Schools / Daycare	☐	☐	☐
Close to Places of Worship	☐	☐	☐
Near Recreational Facilities	☐	☐	☐
Close to Airport	☐	☐	☐
Near Police and Fire Department	☐	☐	☐

31

Address _____   Price _____

Bedrooms _____   Bathrooms _____   Sq.Ft. _____

Lot Size: _____   Year Built _____   School District _____

Annual Tax _____

EXTERIOR

	Good	Average	Poor
View/Yard/Landscaping	☐	☐	☐
Trees	☐	☐	☐
Lawn (Front)	☐	☐	☐
Lawn (Back)	☐	☐	☐
Fences (condition)	☐	☐	☐
Landscaping (condition)	☐	☐	☐
Irrigation / Sprinkler	☐	☐	☐
	☐	☐	☐
House Type	☐	☐	☐
Exterior Siding	☐	☐	☐
Deck / Patio / Porch	☐	☐	☐
Garage	☐	☐	☐
Window / Doors	☐	☐	☐
Roof / Gutters	☐	☐	☐
Fencing	☐	☐	☐

HOME SYSTEMS

	Good	Average	Poor
Electrical	☐	☐	☐
Air Conditioning / Fans	☐	☐	☐
Heating	☐	☐	☐
Security	☐	☐	☐
Plumbing	☐	☐	☐
Intercom	☐	☐	☐

FEATURES

	Good	Average	Poor
Home Warranty	☐	☐	☐
Energy Saving Features	☐	☐	☐

INTERIOR

	Good	Average	Poor
Walls / Trim / Ceilings	☐	☐	☐
Flooring	☐	☐	☐
Stairs	☐	☐	☐
Storage	☐	☐	☐
Living Room	☐	☐	☐
Family Room	☐	☐	☐
Dining Room	☐	☐	☐

	Good	Average	Poor
Master Bedroom	☐	☐	☐
Bedroom 2	☐	☐	☐
Bedroom 3	☐	☐	☐
Bedroom 4	☐	☐	☐
Master Bathroom	☐	☐	☐
Bathroom 2	☐	☐	☐
Bathroom 3	☐	☐	☐
Bonus / Game Room	☐	☐	☐

	Good	Average	Poor
Kitchen	☐	☐	☐
Cabinets	☐	☐	☐
Countertop	☐	☐	☐
Counter Space	☐	☐	☐
Flooring	☐	☐	☐
Oven / Stove	☐	☐	☐
Microwave	☐	☐	☐
Layout	☐	☐	☐
Light Fixtures	☐	☐	☐
Backsplash	☐	☐	☐
Pantry	☐	☐	☐
Appliances	☐	☐	☐
Island	☐	☐	☐

	Good	Average	Poor
Basement	☐	☐	☐
Garage	☐	☐	☐

COMMUNITY

	Good	Average	Poor
Immediate Neighborhood	☐	☐	☐
Close to Employment	☐	☐	☐
Close to Shopping	☐	☐	☐
Close to Transportation	☐	☐	☐
Close to Schools / Daycare	☐	☐	☐
Close to Places of Worship	☐	☐	☐
Near Recreational Facilities	☐	☐	☐
Close to Airport	☐	☐	☐
Near Police and Fire Department	☐	☐	☐

Address _____   Price _____

Bedrooms _____   Bathrooms _____   Sq.Ft. _____

Lot Size: _____   Year Built _____   School District _____

Annual Tax _____

EXTERIOR

	Good	Average	Poor
View/Yard/Landscaping	☐	☐	☐
Trees	☐	☐	☐
Lawn (Front)	☐	☐	☐
Lawn (Back)	☐	☐	☐
Fences (condition)	☐	☐	☐
Landscaping (condition)	☐	☐	☐
Irrigation / Sprinkler	☐	☐	☐
	☐	☐	☐
House Type	☐	☐	☐
Exterior Siding	☐	☐	☐
Deck / Patio / Porch	☐	☐	☐
Garage	☐	☐	☐
Window / Doors	☐	☐	☐
Roof / Gutters	☐	☐	☐
Fencing	☐	☐	☐

HOME SYSTEMS

	Good	Average	Poor
Electrical	☐	☐	☐
Air Conditioning / Fans	☐	☐	☐
Heating	☐	☐	☐
Security	☐	☐	☐
Plumbing	☐	☐	☐
Intercom	☐	☐	☐

FEATURES

	Good	Average	Poor
Home Warranty	☐	☐	☐
Energy Saving Features	☐	☐	☐

INTERIOR

	Good	Average	Poor
Walls / Trim / Ceilings	☐	☐	☐
Flooring	☐	☐	☐
Stairs	☐	☐	☐
Storage	☐	☐	☐
Living Room	☐	☐	☐
Family Room	☐	☐	☐
Dining Room	☐	☐	☐

	Good	Average	Poor
Master Bedroom	☐	☐	☐
Bedroom 2	☐	☐	☐
Bedroom 3	☐	☐	☐
Bedroom 4	☐	☐	☐
Master Bathroom	☐	☐	☐
Bathroom 2	☐	☐	☐
Bathroom 3	☐	☑	☐
Bonus / Game Room	☐	☐	☐

	Good	Average	Poor
Kitchen	☐	☐	☐
Cabinets	☐	☐	☐
Countertop	☐	☐	☐
Counter Space	☐	☐	☐
Flooring	☐	☐	☐
Oven / Stove	☐	☐	☐
Microwave	☐	☐	☐
Layout	☐	☐	☐
Light Fixtures	☐	☐	☐
Backsplash	☐	☐	☐
Pantry	☐	☐	☐
Appliances	☐	☐	☐
Island	☐	☐	☐

	Good	Average	Poor
Basement	☐	☐	☐
Garage	☐	☐	☐

COMMUNITY

	Good	Average	Poor
Immediate Neighborhood	☐	☐	☐
Close to Employment	☐	☐	☐
Close to Shopping	☐	☐	☐
Close to Transportation	☐	☐	☐
Close to Schools / Daycare	☐	☐	☐
Close to Places of Worship	☐	☐	☐
Near Recreational Facilities	☐	☐	☐
Close to Airport	☐	☐	☐
Near Police and Fire Department	☐	☐	☐

Address _____   Price _____

Bedrooms _____   Bathrooms _____   Sq.Ft. _____

Lot Size: _____   Year Built _____   School District _____

Annual Tax _____

EXTERIOR

	Good	Average	Poor
View/Yard/Landscaping	☐	☐	☐
Trees	☐	☐	☐
Lawn (Front)	☐	☐	☐
Lawn (Back)	☐	☐	☐
Fences (condition)	☐	☐	☐
Landscaping (condition)	☐	☐	☐
Irrigation / Sprinkler	☐	☐	☐
	☐	☐	☐
House Type	☐	☐	☐
Exterior Siding	☐	☐	☐
Deck / Patio / Porch	☐	☐	☐
Garage	☐	☐	☐
Window / Doors	☐	☐	☐
Roof / Gutters	☐	☐	☐
Fencing	☐	☐	☐

HOME SYSTEMS

	Good	Average	Poor
Electrical	☐	☐	☐
Air Conditioning / Fans	☐	☐	☐
Heating	☐	☐	☐
Security	☐	☐	☐
Plumbing	☐	☐	☐
Intercom	☐	☐	☐

FEATURES

	Good	Average	Poor
Home Warranty	☐	☐	☐
Energy Saving Features	☐	☐	☐

INTERIOR

	Good	Average	Poor
Walls / Trim / Ceilings	☐	☐	☐
Flooring	☐	☐	☐
Stairs	☐	☐	☐
Storage	☐	☐	☐
Living Room	☐	☐	☐
Family Room	☐	☐	☐
Dining Room	☐	☐	☐

	Good	Average	Poor
Master Bedroom	☐	☐	☐
Bedroom 2	☐	☐	☐
Bedroom 3	☐	☐	☐
Bedroom 4	☐	☐	☐
Master Bathroom	☐	☐	☐
Bathroom 2	☐	☐	☐
Bathroom 3	☐	☐	☐
Bonus / Game Room	☐	☐	☐

	Good	Average	Poor
Kitchen	☐	☐	☐
Cabinets	☐	☐	☐
Countertop	☐	☐	☐
Counter Space	☐	☐	☐
Flooring	☐	☐	☐
Oven / Stove	☐	☐	☐
Microwave	☐	☐	☐
Layout	☐	☐	☐
Light Fixtures	☐	☐	☐
Backsplash	☐	☐	☐
Pantry	☐	☐	☐
Appliances	☐	☐	☐
Island	☐	☐	☐

	Good	Average	Poor
Basement	☐	☐	☐
Garage	☐	☐	☐

COMMUNITY

	Good	Average	Poor
Immediate Neighborhood	☐	☐	☐
Close to Employment	☐	☐	☐
Close to Shopping	☐	☐	☐
Close to Transportation	☐	☐	☐
Close to Schools / Daycare	☐	☐	☐
Close to Places of Worship	☐	☐	☐
Near Recreational Facilities	☐	☐	☐
Close to Airport	☐	☐	☐
Near Police and Fire Department	☐	☐	☐

Address _____   Price _____

Bedrooms _____   Bathrooms _____   Sq.Ft. _____

Lot Size: _____   Year Built _____   School District _____

Annual Tax _____

EXTERIOR

	Good	Average	Poor
View/Yard/Landscaping	☐	☐	☐
Trees	☐	☐	☐
Lawn (Front)	☐	☐	☐
Lawn (Back)	☐	☐	☐
Fences (condition)	☐	☐	☐
Landscaping (condition)	☐	☐	☐
Irrigation / Sprinkler	☐	☐	☐
	☐	☐	☐
House Type	☐	☐	☐
Exterior Siding	☐	☐	☐
Deck / Patio / Porch	☐	☐	☐
Garage	☐	☐	☐
Window / Doors	☐	☐	☐
Roof / Gutters	☐	☐	☐
Fencing	☐	☐	☐

HOME SYSTEMS

	Good	Average	Poor
Electrical	☐	☐	☐
Air Conditioning / Fans	☐	☐	☐
Heating	☐	☐	☐
Security	☐	☐	☐
Plumbing	☐	☐	☐
Intercom	☐	☐	☐

FEATURES

	Good	Average	Poor
Home Warranty	☐	☐	☐
Energy Saving Features	☐	☐	☐

INTERIOR

	Good	Average	Poor
Walls / Trim / Ceilings	☐	☐	☐
Flooring	☐	☐	☐
Stairs	☐	☐	☐
Storage	☐	☐	☐
Living Room	☐	☐	☐
Family Room	☐	☐	☐
Dining Room	☐	☐	☐

	Good	Average	Poor
Master Bedroom	☐	☐	☐
Bedroom 2	☐	☐	☐
Bedroom 3	☐	☐	☐
Bedroom 4	☐	☐	☐
Master Bathroom	☐	☐	☐
Bathroom 2	☐	☐	☐
Bathroom 3	☐	☐	☐
Bonus / Game Room	☐	☐	☐

	Good	Average	Poor
Kitchen	☐	☐	☐
Cabinets	☐	☐	☐
Countertop	☐	☐	☐
Counter Space	☐	☐	☐
Flooring	☐	☐	☐
Oven / Stove	☐	☐	☐
Microwave	☐	☐	☐
Layout	☐	☐	☐
Light Fixtures	☐	☐	☐
Backsplash	☐	☐	☐
Pantry	☐	☐	☐
Appliances	☐	☐	☐
Island	☐	☐	☐

	Good	Average	Poor
Basement	☐	☐	☐
Garage	☐	☐	☐

COMMUNITY

	Good	Average	Poor
Immediate Neighborhood	☐	☐	☐
Close to Employment	☐	☐	☐
Close to Shopping	☐	☐	☐
Close to Transportation	☐	☐	☐
Close to Schools / Daycare	☐	☐	☐
Close to Places of Worship	☐	☐	☐
Near Recreational Facilities	☐	☐	☐
Close to Airport	☐	☐	☐
Near Police and Fire Department	☐	☐	☐

35

Address _____ Price _____

Bedrooms _____ Bathrooms _____ Sq.Ft. _____

Lot Size: _____ Year Built _____ School District _____

Annual Tax _____

EXTERIOR

	Good	Average	Poor
View/Yard/Landscaping	☐	☐	☐
Trees	☐	☐	☐
Lawn (Front)	☐	☐	☐
Lawn (Back)	☐	☐	☐
Fences (condition)	☐	☐	☐
Landscaping (condition)	☐	☐	☐
Irrigation / Sprinkler	☐	☐	☐
	☐	☐	☐
House Type	☐	☐	☐
Exterior Siding	☐	☐	☐
Deck / Patio / Porch	☐	☐	☐
Garage	☐	☐	☐
Window / Doors	☐	☐	☐
Roof / Gutters	☐	☐	☐
Fencing	☐	☐	☐

HOME SYSTEMS

	Good	Average	Poor
Electrical	☐	☐	☐
Air Conditioning / Fans	☐	☐	☐
Heating	☐	☐	☐
Security	☐	☐	☐
Plumbing	☐	☐	☐
Intercom	☐	☐	☐

FEATURES

	Good	Average	Poor
Home Warranty	☐	☐	☐
Energy Saving Features	☐	☐	☐

INTERIOR

	Good	Average	Poor
Walls / Trim / Ceilings	☐	☐	☐
Flooring	☐	☐	☐
Stairs	☐	☐	☐
Storage	☐	☐	☐
Living Room	☐	☐	☐
Family Room	☐	☐	☐
Dining Room	☐	☐	☐

	Good	Average	Poor
Master Bedroom	☐	☐	☐
Bedroom 2	☐	☐	☐
Bedroom 3	☐	☐	☐
Bedroom 4	☐	☐	☐
Master Bathroom	☐	☐	☐
Bathroom 2	☐	☐	☐
Bathroom 3	☐	☐	☐
Bonus / Game Room	☐	☐	☐

	Good	Average	Poor
Kitchen	☐	☐	☐
Cabinets	☐	☐	☐
Countertop	☐	☐	☐
Counter Space	☐	☐	☐
Flooring	☐	☐	☐
Oven / Stove	☐	☐	☐
Microwave	☐	☐	☐
Layout	☐	☐	☐
Light Fixtures	☐	☐	☐
Backsplash	☐	☐	☐
Pantry	☐	☐	☐
Appliances	☐	☐	☐
Island	☐	☐	☐

	Good	Average	Poor
Basement	☐	☐	☐
Garage	☐	☐	☐

COMMUNITY

	Good	Average	Poor
Immediate Neighborhood	☐	☐	☐
Close to Employment	☐	☐	☐
Close to Shopping	☐	☐	☐
Close to Transportation	☐	☐	☐
Close to Schools / Daycare	☐	☐	☐
Close to Places of Worship	☐	☐	☐
Near Recreational Facilities	☐	☐	☐
Close to Airport	☐	☐	☐
Near Police and Fire Department	☐	☐	☐

Address _____   Price _____

Bedrooms _____   Bathrooms _____   Sq.Ft. _____

Lot Size: _____   Year Built _____   School District _____

Annual Tax _____

EXTERIOR

	Good	Average	Poor
View/Yard/Landscaping	☐	☐	☐
Trees	☐	☐	☐
Lawn (Front)	☐	☐	☐
Lawn (Back)	☐	☐	☐
Fences (condition)	☐	☐	☐
Landscaping (condition)	☐	☐	☐
Irrigation / Sprinkler	☐	☐	☐
	☐	☐	☐
House Type	☐	☐	☐
Exterior Siding	☐	☐	☐
Deck / Patio / Porch	☐	☐	☐
Garage	☐	☐	☐
Window / Doors	☐	☐	☐
Roof / Gutters	☐	☐	☐
Fencing	☐	☐	☐

HOME SYSTEMS

	Good	Average	Poor
Electrical	☐	☐	☐
Air Conditioning / Fans	☐	☐	☐
Heating	☐	☐	☐
Security	☐	☐	☐
Plumbing	☐	☐	☐
Intercom	☐	☐	☐

FEATURES

	Good	Average	Poor
Home Warranty	☐	☐	☐
Energy Saving Features	☐	☐	☐

INTERIOR

	Good	Average	Poor
Walls / Trim / Ceilings	☐	☐	☐
Flooring	☐	☐	☐
Stairs	☐	☐	☐
Storage	☐	☐	☐
Living Room	☐	☐	☐
Family Room	☐	☐	☐
Dining Room	☐	☐	☐

	Good	Average	Poor
Master Bedroom	☐	☐	☐
Bedroom 2	☐	☐	☐
Bedroom 3	☐	☐	☐
Bedroom 4	☐	☐	☐
Master Bathroom	☐	☐	☐
Bathroom 2	☐	☐	☐
Bathroom 3	☐	☐	☐
Bonus / Game Room	☐	☐	☐

	Good	Average	Poor
Kitchen	☐	☐	☐
Cabinets	☐	☐	☐
Countertop	☐	☐	☐
Counter Space	☐	☐	☐
Flooring	☐	☐	☐
Oven / Stove	☐	☐	☐
Microwave	☐	☐	☐
Layout	☐	☐	☐
Light Fixtures	☐	☐	☐
Backsplash	☐	☐	☐
Pantry	☐	☐	☐
Appliances	☐	☐	☐
Island	☐	☐	☐

	Good	Average	Poor
Basement	☐	☐	☐
Garage	☐	☐	☐

COMMUNITY

	Good	Average	Poor
Immediate Neighborhood	☐	☐	☐
Close to Employment	☐	☐	☐
Close to Shopping	☐	☐	☐
Close to Transportation	☐	☐	☐
Close to Schools / Daycare	☐	☐	☐
Close to Places of Worship	☐	☐	☐
Near Recreational Facilities	☐	☐	☐
Close to Airport	☐	☐	☐
Near Police and Fire Department	☐	☐	☐

Address _____ Price _____

Bedrooms _____ Bathrooms _____ Sq.Ft. _____

Lot Size: _____ Year Built _____ School District _____

Annual Tax _____

EXTERIOR

	Good	Average	Poor
View/Yard/Landscaping	☐	☐	☐
Trees	☐	☐	☐
Lawn (Front)	☐	☐	☐
Lawn (Back)	☐	☐	☐
Fences (condition)	☐	☐	☐
Landscaping (condition)	☐	☐	☐
Irrigation / Sprinkler	☐	☐	☐
	☐	☐	☐
House Type	☐	☐	☐
Exterior Siding	☐	☐	☐
Deck / Patio / Porch	☐	☐	☐
Garage	☐	☐	☐
Window / Doors	☐	☐	☐
Roof / Gutters	☐	☐	☐
Fencing	☐	☐	☐

HOME SYSTEMS

	Good	Average	Poor
Electrical	☐	☐	☐
Air Conditioning / Fans	☐	☐	☐
Heating	☐	☐	☐
Security	☐	☐	☐
Plumbing	☐	☐	☐
Intercom	☐	☐	☐

FEATURES

	Good	Average	Poor
Home Warranty	☐	☐	☐
Energy Saving Features	☐	☐	☐

INTERIOR

	Good	Average	Poor
Walls / Trim / Ceilings	☐	☐	☐
Flooring	☐	☐	☐
Stairs	☐	☐	☐
Storage	☐	☐	☐
Living Room	☐	☐	☐
Family Room	☐	☐	☐
Dining Room	☐	☐	☐

	Good	Average	Poor
Master Bedroom	☐	☐	☐
Bedroom 2	☐	☐	☐
Bedroom 3	☐	☐	☐
Bedroom 4	☐	☐	☐
Master Bathroom	☐	☐	☐
Bathroom 2	☐	☐	☐
Bathroom 3	☐	☐	☐
Bonus / Game Room	☐	☐	☐

	Good	Average	Poor
Kitchen	☐	☐	☐
Cabinets	☐	☐	☐
Countertop	☐	☐	☐
Counter Space	☐	☐	☐
Flooring	☐	☐	☐
Oven / Stove	☐	☐	☐
Microwave	☐	☐	☐
Layout	☐	☐	☐
Light Fixtures	☐	☐	☐
Backsplash	☐	☐	☐
Pantry	☐	☐	☐
Appliances	☐	☐	☐
Island	☐	☐	☐

	Good	Average	Poor
Basement	☐	☐	☐
Garage	☐	☐	☐

COMMUNITY

	Good	Average	Poor
Immediate Neighborhood	☐	☐	☐
Close to Employment	☐	☐	☐
Close to Shopping	☐	☐	☐
Close to Transportation	☐	☐	☐
Close to Schools / Daycare	☐	☐	☐
Close to Places of Worship	☐	☐	☐
Near Recreational Facilities	☐	☐	☐
Close to Airport	☐	☐	☐
Near Police and Fire Department	☐	☐	☐

Address _____ Price _____

Bedrooms _____ Bathrooms _____ Sq.Ft. _____

Lot Size: _____ Year Built _____ School District _____

Annual Tax _____

EXTERIOR

	Good	Average	Poor
View/Yard/Landscaping	☐	☐	☐
Trees	☐	☐	☐
Lawn (Front)	☐	☐	☐
Lawn (Back)	☐	☐	☐
Fences (condition)	☐	☐	☐
Landscaping (condition)	☐	☐	☐
Irrigation / Sprinkler	☐	☐	☐
	☐	☐	☐
House Type	☐	☐	☐
Exterior Siding	☐	☐	☐
Deck / Patio / Porch	☐	☐	☐
Garage	☐	☐	☐
Window / Doors	☐	☐	☐
Roof / Gutters	☐	☐	☐
Fencing	☐	☐	☐

HOME SYSTEMS

	Good	Average	Poor
Electrical	☐	☐	☐
Air Conditioning / Fans	☐	☐	☐
Heating	☐	☐	☐
Security	☐	☐	☐
Plumbing	☐	☐	☐
Intercom	☐	☐	☐

FEATURES

	Good	Average	Poor
Home Warranty	☐	☐	☐
Energy Saving Features	☐	☐	☐

INTERIOR

	Good	Average	Poor
Walls / Trim / Ceilings	☐	☐	☐
Flooring	☐	☐	☐
Stairs	☐	☐	☐
Storage	☐	☐	☐
Living Room	☐	☐	☐
Family Room	☐	☐	☐
Dining Room	☐	☐	☐

	Good	Average	Poor
Master Bedroom	☐	☐	☐
Bedroom 2	☐	☐	☐
Bedroom 3	☐	☐	☐
Bedroom 4	☐	☐	☐
Master Bathroom	☐	☐	☐
Bathroom 2	☐	☐	☐
Bathroom 3	☐	☑	☐
Bonus / Game Room	☐	☐	☐

	Good	Average	Poor
Kitchen	☐	☐	☐
Cabinets	☐	☐	☐
Countertop	☐	☐	☐
Counter Space	☐	☐	☐
Flooring	☐	☐	☐
Oven / Stove	☐	☐	☐
Microwave	☐	☐	☐
Layout	☐	☐	☐
Light Fixtures	☐	☐	☐
Backsplash	☐	☐	☐
Pantry	☐	☐	☐
Appliances	☐	☐	☐
Island	☐	☐	☐

	Good	Average	Poor
Basement	☐	☐	☐
Garage	☐	☐	☐

COMMUNITY

	Good	Average	Poor
Immediate Neighborhood	☐	☐	☐
Close to Employment	☐	☐	☐
Close to Shopping	☐	☐	☐
Close to Transportation	☐	☐	☐
Close to Schools / Daycare	☐	☐	☐
Close to Places of Worship	☐	☐	☐
Near Recreational Facilities	☐	☐	☐
Close to Airport	☐	☐	☐
Near Police and Fire Department	☐	☐	☐

39

Address _____   Price _____

Bedrooms _____   Bathrooms _____   Sq.Ft. _____

Lot Size: _____   Year Built _____   School District _____

Annual Tax _____

EXTERIOR

	Good	Average	Poor
View/Yard/Landscaping	☐	☐	☐
Trees	☐	☐	☐
Lawn (Front)	☐	☐	☐
Lawn (Back)	☐	☐	☐
Fences (condition)	☐	☐	☐
Landscaping (condition)	☐	☐	☐
Irrigation / Sprinkler	☐	☐	☐
	☐	☐	☐
House Type	☐	☐	☐
Exterior Siding	☐	☐	☐
Deck / Patio / Porch	☐	☐	☐
Garage	☐	☐	☐
Window / Doors	☐	☐	☐
Roof / Gutters	☐	☐	☐
Fencing	☐	☐	☐

HOME SYSTEMS

	Good	Average	Poor
Electrical	☐	☐	☐
Air Conditioning / Fans	☐	☐	☐
Heating	☐	☐	☐
Security	☐	☐	☐
Plumbing	☐	☐	☐
Intercom	☐	☐	☐

FEATURES

	Good	Average	Poor
Home Warranty	☐	☐	☐
Energy Saving Features	☐	☐	☐

INTERIOR

	Good	Average	Poor
Walls / Trim / Ceilings	☐	☐	☐
Flooring	☐	☐	☐
Stairs	☐	☐	☐
Storage	☐	☐	☐
Living Room	☐	☐	☐
Family Room	☐	☐	☐
Dining Room	☐	☐	☐

	Good	Average	Poor
Master Bedroom	☐	☐	☐
Bedroom 2	☐	☐	☐
Bedroom 3	☐	☐	☐
Bedroom 4	☐	☐	☐
Master Bathroom	☐	☐	☐
Bathroom 2	☐	☐	☐
Bathroom 3	☐	☐	☐
Bonus / Game Room	☐	☐	☐

	Good	Average	Poor
Kitchen	☐	☐	☐
Cabinets	☐	☐	☐
Countertop	☐	☐	☐
Counter Space	☐	☐	☐
Flooring	☐	☐	☐
Oven / Stove	☐	☐	☐
Microwave	☐	☐	☐
Layout	☐	☐	☐
Light Fixtures	☐	☐	☐
Backsplash	☐	☐	☐
Pantry	☐	☐	☐
Appliances	☐	☐	☐
Island	☐	☐	☐

	Good	Average	Poor
Basement	☐	☐	☐
Garage	☐	☐	☐

COMMUNITY

	Good	Average	Poor
Immediate Neighborhood	☐	☐	☐
Close to Employment	☐	☐	☐
Close to Shopping	☐	☐	☐
Close to Transportation	☐	☐	☐
Close to Schools / Daycare	☐	☐	☐
Close to Places of Worship	☐	☐	☐
Near Recreational Facilities	☐	☐	☐
Close to Airport	☐	☐	☐
Near Police and Fire Department	☐	☐	☐

40

Address _____   Price _____

Bedrooms _____   Bathrooms _____   Sq.Ft. _____

Lot Size: _____   Year Built _____   School District _____

Annual Tax _____

EXTERIOR

	Good	Average	Poor
View/Yard/Landscaping	☐	☐	☐
Trees	☐	☐	☐
Lawn (Front)	☐	☐	☐
Lawn (Back)	☐	☐	☐
Fences (condition)	☐	☐	☐
Landscaping (condition)	☐	☐	☐
Irrigation / Sprinkler	☐	☐	☐
	☐	☐	☐
House Type	☐	☐	☐
Exterior Siding	☐	☐	☐
Deck / Patio / Porch	☐	☐	☐
Garage	☐	☐	☐
Window / Doors	☐	☐	☐
Roof / Gutters	☐	☐	☐
Fencing	☐	☐	☐

HOME SYSTEMS

	Good	Average	Poor
Electrical	☐	☐	☐
Air Conditioning / Fans	☐	☐	☐
Heating	☐	☐	☐
Security	☐	☐	☐
Plumbing	☐	☐	☐
Intercom	☐	☐	☐

FEATURES

	Good	Average	Poor
Home Warranty	☐	☐	☐
Energy Saving Features	☐	☐	☐

INTERIOR

	Good	Average	Poor
Walls / Trim / Ceilings	☐	☐	☐
Flooring	☐	☐	☐
Stairs	☐	☐	☐
Storage	☐	☐	☐
Living Room	☐	☐	☐
Family Room	☐	☐	☐
Dining Room	☐	☐	☐

	Good	Average	Poor
Master Bedroom	☐	☐	☐
Bedroom 2	☐	☐	☐
Bedroom 3	☐	☐	☐
Bedroom 4	☐	☐	☐
Master Bathroom	☐	☐	☐
Bathroom 2	☐	☐	☐
Bathroom 3	☐	☐	☐
Bonus / Game Room	☐	☐	☐

	Good	Average	Poor
Kitchen	☐	☐	☐
Cabinets	☐	☐	☐
Countertop	☐	☐	☐
Counter Space	☐	☐	☐
Flooring	☐	☐	☐
Oven / Stove	☐	☐	☐
Microwave	☐	☐	☐
Layout	☐	☐	☐
Light Fixtures	☐	☐	☐
Backsplash	☐	☐	☐
Pantry	☐	☐	☐
Appliances	☐	☐	☐
Island	☐	☐	☐

	Good	Average	Poor
Basement	☐	☐	☐
Garage	☐	☐	☐

COMMUNITY

	Good	Average	Poor
Immediate Neighborhood	☐	☐	☐
Close to Employment	☐	☐	☐
Close to Shopping	☐	☐	☐
Close to Transportation	☐	☐	☐
Close to Schools / Daycare	☐	☐	☐
Close to Places of Worship	☐	☐	☐
Near Recreational Facilities	☐	☐	☐
Close to Airport	☐	☐	☐
Near Police and Fire Department	☐	☐	☐

Address _____   Price _____

Bedrooms _____ Bathrooms _____ Sq.Ft. _____

Lot Size: _____ Year Built _____ School District _____

Annual Tax _____

EXTERIOR

	Good	Average	Poor
View/Yard/Landscaping	☐	☐	☐
Trees	☐	☐	☐
Lawn (Front)	☐	☐	☐
Lawn (Back)	☐	☐	☐
Fences (condition)	☐	☐	☐
Landscaping (condition)	☐	☐	☐
Irrigation / Sprinkler	☐	☐	☐
	☐	☐	☐
House Type	☐	☐	☐
Exterior Siding	☐	☐	☐
Deck / Patio / Porch	☐	☐	☐
Garage	☐	☐	☐
Window / Doors	☐	☐	☐
Roof / Gutters	☐	☐	☐
Fencing	☐	☐	☐

HOME SYSTEMS

	Good	Average	Poor
Electrical	☐	☐	☐
Air Conditioning / Fans	☐	☐	☐
Heating	☐	☐	☐
Security	☐	☐	☐
Plumbing	☐	☐	☐
Intercom	☐	☐	☐

FEATURES

	Good	Average	Poor
Home Warranty	☐	☐	☐
Energy Saving Features	☐	☐	☐

INTERIOR

	Good	Average	Poor
Walls / Trim / Ceilings	☐	☐	☐
Flooring	☐	☐	☐
Stairs	☐	☐	☐
Storage	☐	☐	☐
Living Room	☐	☐	☐
Family Room	☐	☐	☐
Dining Room	☐	☐	☐

	Good	Average	Poor
Master Bedroom	☐	☐	☐
Bedroom 2	☐	☐	☐
Bedroom 3	☐	☐	☐
Bedroom 4	☐	☐	☐
Master Bathroom	☐	☐	☐
Bathroom 2	☐	☐	☐
Bathroom 3	☐	☐	☐
Bonus / Game Room	☐	☐	☐

	Good	Average	Poor
Kitchen	☐	☐	☐
Cabinets	☐	☐	☐
Countertop	☐	☐	☐
Counter Space	☐	☐	☐
Flooring	☐	☐	☐
Oven / Stove	☐	☐	☐
Microwave	☐	☐	☐
Layout	☐	☐	☐
Light Fixtures	☐	☐	☐
Backsplash	☐	☐	☐
Pantry	☐	☐	☐
Appliances	☐	☐	☐
Island	☐	☐	☐

	Good	Average	Poor
Basement	☐	☐	☐
Garage	☐	☐	☐

COMMUNITY

	Good	Average	Poor
Immediate Neighborhood	☐	☐	☐
Close to Employment	☐	☐	☐
Close to Shopping	☐	☐	☐
Close to Transportation	☐	☐	☐
Close to Schools / Daycare	☐	☐	☐
Close to Places of Worship	☐	☐	☐
Near Recreational Facilities	☐	☐	☐
Close to Airport	☐	☐	☐
Near Police and Fire Department	☐	☐	☐

Address _____   Price _____

Bedrooms _____   Bathrooms _____   Sq.Ft. _____

Lot Size: _____   Year Built _____   School District _____

Annual Tax _____

EXTERIOR

	Good	Average	Poor
View/Yard/Landscaping	☐	☐	☐
Trees	☐	☐	☐
Lawn (Front)	☐	☐	☐
Lawn (Back)	☐	☐	☐
Fences (condition)	☐	☐	☐
Landscaping (condition)	☐	☐	☐
Irrigation / Sprinkler	☐	☐	☐
	☐	☐	☐
House Type	☐	☐	☐
Exterior Siding	☐	☐	☐
Deck / Patio / Porch	☐	☐	☐
Garage	☐	☐	☐
Window / Doors	☐	☐	☐
Roof / Gutters	☐	☐	☐
Fencing	☐	☐	☐

HOME SYSTEMS

	Good	Average	Poor
Electrical	☐	☐	☐
Air Conditioning / Fans	☐	☐	☐
Heating	☐	☐	☐
Security	☐	☐	☐
Plumbing	☐	☐	☐
Intercom	☐	☐	☐

FEATURES

	Good	Average	Poor
Home Warranty	☐	☐	☐
Energy Saving Features	☐	☐	☐

INTERIOR

	Good	Average	Poor
Walls / Trim / Ceilings	☐	☐	☐
Flooring	☐	☐	☐
Stairs	☐	☐	☐
Storage	☐	☐	☐
Living Room	☐	☐	☐
Family Room	☐	☐	☐
Dining Room	☐	☐	☐

	Good	Average	Poor
Master Bedroom	☐	☐	☐
Bedroom 2	☐	☐	☐
Bedroom 3	☐	☐	☐
Bedroom 4	☐	☐	☐
Master Bathroom	☐	☐	☐
Bathroom 2	☐	☐	☐
Bathroom 3	☐	☐	☐
Bonus / Game Room	☐	☐	☐

	Good	Average	Poor
Kitchen	☐	☐	☐
Cabinets	☐	☐	☐
Countertop	☐	☐	☐
Counter Space	☐	☐	☐
Flooring	☐	☐	☐
Oven / Stove	☐	☐	☐
Microwave	☐	☐	☐
Layout	☐	☐	☐
Light Fixtures	☐	☐	☐
Backsplash	☐	☐	☐
Pantry	☐	☐	☐
Appliances	☐	☐	☐
Island	☐	☐	☐

	Good	Average	Poor
Basement	☐	☐	☐
Garage	☐	☐	☐

COMMUNITY

	Good	Average	Poor
Immediate Neighborhood	☐	☐	☐
Close to Employment	☐	☐	☐
Close to Shopping	☐	☐	☐
Close to Transportation	☐	☐	☐
Close to Schools / Daycare	☐	☐	☐
Close to Places of Worship	☐	☐	☐
Near Recreational Facilities	☐	☐	☐
Close to Airport	☐	☐	☐
Near Police and Fire Department	☐	☐	☐

Address _____ Price _____

Bedrooms _____ Bathrooms _____ Sq.Ft. _____

Lot Size: _____ Year Built _____ School District _____

Annual Tax _____

EXTERIOR

	Good	Average	Poor
View/Yard/Landscaping	☐	☐	☐
Trees	☐	☐	☐
Lawn (Front)	☐	☐	☐
Lawn (Back)	☐	☐	☐
Fences (condition)	☐	☐	☐
Landscaping (condition)	☐	☐	☐
Irrigation / Sprinkler	☐	☐	☐
	☐	☐	☐
House Type	☐	☐	☐
Exterior Siding	☐	☐	☐
Deck / Patio / Porch	☐	☐	☐
Garage	☐	☐	☐
Window / Doors	☐	☐	☐
Roof / Gutters	☐	☐	☐
Fencing	☐	☐	☐

HOME SYSTEMS

	Good	Average	Poor
Electrical	☐	☐	☐
Air Conditioning / Fans	☐	☐	☐
Heating	☐	☐	☐
Security	☐	☐	☐
Plumbing	☐	☐	☐
Intercom	☐	☐	☐

FEATURES

	Good	Average	Poor
Home Warranty	☐	☐	☐
Energy Saving Features	☐	☐	☐

INTERIOR

	Good	Average	Poor
Walls / Trim / Ceilings	☐	☐	☐
Flooring	☐	☐	☐
Stairs	☐	☐	☐
Storage	☐	☐	☐
Living Room	☐	☐	☐
Family Room	☐	☐	☐
Dining Room	☐	☐	☐

	Good	Average	Poor
Master Bedroom	☐	☐	☐
Bedroom 2	☐	☐	☐
Bedroom 3	☐	☐	☐
Bedroom 4	☐	☐	☐
Master Bathroom	☐	☐	☐
Bathroom 2	☐	☐	☐
Bathroom 3	☐	☐	☐
Bonus / Game Room	☐	☐	☐

	Good	Average	Poor
Kitchen	☐	☐	☐
Cabinets	☐	☐	☐
Countertop	☐	☐	☐
Counter Space	☐	☐	☐
Flooring	☐	☐	☐
Oven / Stove	☐	☐	☐
Microwave	☐	☐	☐
Layout	☐	☐	☐
Light Fixtures	☐	☐	☐
Backsplash	☐	☐	☐
Pantry	☐	☐	☐
Appliances	☐	☐	☐
Island	☐	☐	☐

	Good	Average	Poor
Basement	☐	☐	☐
Garage	☐	☐	☐

COMMUNITY

	Good	Average	Poor
Immediate Neighborhood	☐	☐	☐
Close to Employment	☐	☐	☐
Close to Shopping	☐	☐	☐
Close to Transportation	☐	☐	☐
Close to Schools / Daycare	☐	☐	☐
Close to Places of Worship	☐	☐	☐
Near Recreational Facilities	☐	☐	☐
Close to Airport	☐	☐	☐
Near Police and Fire Department	☐	☐	☐

Address _____   Price _____

Bedrooms _____   Bathrooms _____   Sq.Ft. _____

Lot Size: _____   Year Built _____   School District _____

Annual Tax _____

EXTERIOR

	Good	Average	Poor
View/Yard/Landscaping	☐	☐	☐
Trees	☐	☐	☐
Lawn (Front)	☐	☐	☐
Lawn (Back)	☐	☐	☐
Fences (condition)	☐	☐	☐
Landscaping (condition)	☐	☐	☐
Irrigation / Sprinkler	☐	☐	☐
	☐	☐	☐
House Type	☐	☐	☐
Exterior Siding	☐	☐	☐
Deck / Patio / Porch	☐	☐	☐
Garage	☐	☐	☐
Window / Doors	☐	☐	☐
Roof / Gutters	☐	☐	☐
Fencing	☐	☐	☐

HOME SYSTEMS

	Good	Average	Poor
Electrical	☐	☐	☐
Air Conditioning / Fans	☐	☐	☐
Heating	☐	☐	☐
Security	☐	☐	☐
Plumbing	☐	☐	☐
Intercom	☐	☐	☐

FEATURES

	Good	Average	Poor
Home Warranty	☐	☐	☐
Energy Saving Features	☐	☐	☐

INTERIOR

	Good	Average	Poor
Walls / Trim / Ceilings	☐	☐	☐
Flooring	☐	☐	☐
Stairs	☐	☐	☐
Storage	☐	☐	☐
Living Room	☐	☐	☐
Family Room	☐	☐	☐
Dining Room	☐	☐	☐

	Good	Average	Poor
Master Bedroom	☐	☐	☐
Bedroom 2	☐	☐	☐
Bedroom 3	☐	☐	☐
Bedroom 4	☐	☐	☐
Master Bathroom	☐	☐	☐
Bathroom 2	☐	☐	☐
Bathroom 3	☐	☐	☐
Bonus / Game Room	☐	☐	☐

	Good	Average	Poor
Kitchen	☐	☐	☐
Cabinets	☐	☐	☐
Countertop	☐	☐	☐
Counter Space	☐	☐	☐
Flooring	☐	☐	☐
Oven / Stove	☐	☐	☐
Microwave	☐	☐	☐
Layout	☐	☐	☐
Light Fixtures	☐	☐	☐
Backsplash	☐	☐	☐
Pantry	☐	☐	☐
Appliances	☐	☐	☐
Island	☐	☐	☐

	Good	Average	Poor
Basement	☐	☐	☐
Garage	☐	☐	☐

COMMUNITY

	Good	Average	Poor
Immediate Neighborhood	☐	☐	☐
Close to Employment	☐	☐	☐
Close to Shopping	☐	☐	☐
Close to Transportation	☐	☐	☐
Close to Schools / Daycare	☐	☐	☐
Close to Places of Worship	☐	☐	☐
Near Recreational Facilities	☐	☐	☐
Close to Airport	☐	☐	☐
Near Police and Fire Department	☐	☐	☐

Address _____   Price _____

Bedrooms _____   Bathrooms _____   Sq.Ft. _____

Lot Size: _____   Year Built _____   School District _____

Annual Tax _____

EXTERIOR

	Good	Average	Poor
View/Yard/Landscaping	☐	☐	☐
Trees	☐	☐	☐
Lawn (Front)	☐	☐	☐
Lawn (Back)	☐	☐	☐
Fences (condition)	☐	☐	☐
Landscaping (condition)	☐	☐	☐
Irrigation / Sprinkler	☐	☐	☐
	☐	☐	☐
House Type	☐	☐	☐
Exterior Siding	☐	☐	☐
Deck / Patio / Porch	☐	☐	☐
Garage	☐	☐	☐
Window / Doors	☐	☐	☐
Roof / Gutters	☐	☐	☐
Fencing	☐	☐	☐

HOME SYSTEMS

	Good	Average	Poor
Electrical	☐	☐	☐
Air Conditioning / Fans	☐	☐	☐
Heating	☐	☐	☐
Security	☐	☐	☐
Plumbing	☐	☐	☐
Intercom	☐	☐	☐

FEATURES

	Good	Average	Poor
Home Warranty	☐	☐	☐
Energy Saving Features	☐	☐	☐

INTERIOR

	Good	Average	Poor
Walls / Trim / Ceilings	☐	☐	☐
Flooring	☐	☐	☐
Stairs	☐	☐	☐
Storage	☐	☐	☐
Living Room	☐	☐	☐
Family Room	☐	☐	☐
Dining Room	☐	☐	☐

	Good	Average	Poor
Master Bedroom	☐	☐	☐
Bedroom 2	☐	☐	☐
Bedroom 3	☐	☐	☐
Bedroom 4	☐	☐	☐
Master Bathroom	☐	☐	☐
Bathroom 2	☐	☐	☐
Bathroom 3	☐	☐	☐
Bonus / Game Room	☐	☐	☐

	Good	Average	Poor
Kitchen	☐	☐	☐
Cabinets	☐	☐	☐
Countertop	☐	☐	☐
Counter Space	☐	☐	☐
Flooring	☐	☐	☐
Oven / Stove	☐	☐	☐
Microwave	☐	☐	☐
Layout	☐	☐	☐
Light Fixtures	☐	☐	☐
Backsplash	☐	☐	☐
Pantry	☐	☐	☐
Appliances	☐	☐	☐
Island	☐	☐	☐

	Good	Average	Poor
Basement	☐	☐	☐
Garage	☐	☐	☐

COMMUNITY

	Good	Average	Poor
Immediate Neighborhood	☐	☐	☐
Close to Employment	☐	☐	☐
Close to Shopping	☐	☐	☐
Close to Transportation	☐	☐	☐
Close to Schools / Daycare	☐	☐	☐
Close to Places of Worship	☐	☐	☐
Near Recreational Facilities	☐	☐	☐
Close to Airport	☐	☐	☐
Near Police and Fire Department	☐	☐	☐

46

Address _____ Price _____

Bedrooms _____ Bathrooms _____ Sq.Ft. _____

Lot Size: _____ Year Built _____ School District _____

Annual Tax _____

EXTERIOR

	Good	Average	Poor
View/Yard/Landscaping	☐	☐	☐
Trees	☐	☐	☐
Lawn (Front)	☐	☐	☐
Lawn (Back)	☐	☐	☐
Fences (condition)	☐	☐	☐
Landscaping (condition)	☐	☐	☐
Irrigation / Sprinkler	☐	☐	☐
	☐	☐	☐
House Type	☐	☐	☐
Exterior Siding	☐	☐	☐
Deck / Patio / Porch	☐	☐	☐
Garage	☐	☐	☐
Window / Doors	☐	☐	☐
Roof / Gutters	☐	☐	☐
Fencing	☐	☐	☐

	Good	Average	Poor
Master Bedroom	☐	☐	☐
Bedroom 2	☐	☐	☐
Bedroom 3	☐	☐	☐
Bedroom 4	☐	☐	☐
Master Bathroom	☐	☐	☐
Bathroom 2	☐	☐	☐
Bathroom 3	☐	☐	☐
Bonus / Game Room	☐	☐	☐

	Good	Average	Poor
Kitchen	☐	☐	☐
Cabinets	☐	☐	☐
Countertop	☐	☐	☐
Counter Space	☐	☐	☐
Flooring	☐	☐	☐
Oven / Stove	☐	☐	☐
Microwave	☐	☐	☐
Layout	☐	☐	☐
Light Fixtures	☐	☐	☐
Backsplash	☐	☐	☐
Pantry	☐	☐	☐
Appliances	☐	☐	☐
Island	☐	☐	☐

HOME SYSTEMS

	Good	Average	Poor
Electrical	☐	☐	☐
Air Conditioning / Fans	☐	☐	☐
Heating	☐	☐	☐
Security	☐	☐	☐
Plumbing	☐	☐	☐
Intercom	☐	☐	☐

	Good	Average	Poor
Basement	☐	☐	☐
Garage	☐	☐	☐

FEATURES

	Good	Average	Poor
Home Warranty	☐	☐	☐
Energy Saving Features	☐	☐	☐

INTERIOR

	Good	Average	Poor
Walls / Trim / Ceilings	☐	☐	☐
Flooring	☐	☐	☐
Stairs	☐	☐	☐
Storage	☐	☐	☐
Living Room	☐	☐	☐
Family Room	☐	☐	☐
Dining Room	☐	☐	☐

COMMUNITY

	Good	Average	Poor
Immediate Neighborhood	☐	☐	☐
Close to Employment	☐	☐	☐
Close to Shopping	☐	☐	☐
Close to Transportation	☐	☐	☐
Close to Schools / Daycare	☐	☐	☐
Close to Places of Worship	☐	☐	☐
Near Recreational Facilities	☐	☐	☐
Close to Airport	☐	☐	☐
Near Police and Fire Department	☐	☐	☐

Address _____   Price _____

Bedrooms _____ Bathrooms _____ Sq.Ft. _____

Lot Size: _____ Year Built _____ School District _____

Annual Tax _____

EXTERIOR

	Good	Average	Poor
View/Yard/Landscaping	☐	☐	☐
Trees	☐	☐	☐
Lawn (Front)	☐	☐	☐
Lawn (Back)	☐	☐	☐
Fences (condition)	☐	☐	☐
Landscaping (condition)	☐	☐	☐
Irrigation / Sprinkler	☐	☐	☐
	☐	☐	☐
House Type	☐	☐	☐
Exterior Siding	☐	☐	☐
Deck / Patio / Porch	☐	☐	☐
Garage	☐	☐	☐
Window / Doors	☐	☐	☐
Roof / Gutters	☐	☐	☐
Fencing	☐	☐	☐

HOME SYSTEMS

	Good	Average	Poor
Electrical	☐	☐	☐
Air Conditioning / Fans	☐	☐	☐
Heating	☐	☐	☐
Security	☐	☐	☐
Plumbing	☐	☐	☐
Intercom	☐	☐	☐

FEATURES

	Good	Average	Poor
Home Warranty	☐	☐	☐
Energy Saving Features	☐	☐	☐

INTERIOR

	Good	Average	Poor
Walls / Trim / Ceilings	☐	☐	☐
Flooring	☐	☐	☐
Stairs	☐	☐	☐
Storage	☐	☐	☐
Living Room	☐	☐	☐
Family Room	☐	☐	☐
Dining Room	☐	☐	☐

	Good	Average	Poor
Master Bedroom	☐	☐	☐
Bedroom 2	☐	☐	☐
Bedroom 3	☐	☐	☐
Bedroom 4	☐	☐	☐
Master Bathroom	☐	☐	☐
Bathroom 2	☐	☐	☐
Bathroom 3	☐	☐	☐
Bonus / Game Room	☐	☐	☐

	Good	Average	Poor
Kitchen	☐	☐	☐
Cabinets	☐	☐	☐
Countertop	☐	☐	☐
Counter Space	☐	☐	☐
Flooring	☐	☐	☐
Oven / Stove	☐	☐	☐
Microwave	☐	☐	☐
Layout	☐	☐	☐
Light Fixtures	☐	☐	☐
Backsplash	☐	☐	☐
Pantry	☐	☐	☐
Appliances	☐	☐	☐
Island	☐	☐	☐

	Good	Average	Poor
Basement	☐	☐	☐
Garage	☐	☐	☐

COMMUNITY

	Good	Average	Poor
Immediate Neighborhood	☐	☐	☐
Close to Employment	☐	☐	☐
Close to Shopping	☐	☐	☐
Close to Transportation	☐	☐	☐
Close to Schools / Daycare	☐	☐	☐
Close to Places of Worship	☐	☐	☐
Near Recreational Facilities	☐	☐	☐
Close to Airport	☐	☐	☐
Near Police and Fire Department	☐	☐	☐

Address _____ Price _____

Bedrooms _____ Bathrooms _____ Sq.Ft. _____

Lot Size: _____ Year Built _____ School District _____

Annual Tax _____

EXTERIOR

	Good	Average	Poor
View/Yard/Landscaping	☐	☐	☐
Trees	☐	☐	☐
Lawn (Front)	☐	☐	☐
Lawn (Back)	☐	☐	☐
Fences (condition)	☐	☐	☐
Landscaping (condition)	☐	☐	☐
Irrigation / Sprinkler	☐	☐	☐
	☐	☐	☐
House Type	☐	☐	☐
Exterior Siding	☐	☐	☐
Deck / Patio / Porch	☐	☐	☐
Garage	☐	☐	☐
Window / Doors	☐	☐	☐
Roof / Gutters	☐	☐	☐
Fencing	☐	☐	☐

HOME SYSTEMS

	Good	Average	Poor
Electrical	☐	☐	☐
Air Conditioning / Fans	☐	☐	☐
Heating	☐	☐	☐
Security	☐	☐	☐
Plumbing	☐	☐	☐
Intercom	☐	☐	☐

FEATURES

	Good	Average	Poor
Home Warranty	☐	☐	☐
Energy Saving Features	☐	☐	☐

INTERIOR

	Good	Average	Poor
Walls / Trim / Ceilings	☐	☐	☐
Flooring	☐	☐	☐
Stairs	☐	☐	☐
Storage	☐	☐	☐
Living Room	☐	☐	☐
Family Room	☐	☐	☐
Dining Room	☐	☐	☐

	Good	Average	Poor
Master Bedroom	☐	☐	☐
Bedroom 2	☐	☐	☐
Bedroom 3	☐	☐	☐
Bedroom 4	☐	☐	☐
Master Bathroom	☐	☐	☐
Bathroom 2	☐	☐	☐
Bathroom 3	☐	☐	☐
Bonus / Game Room	☐	☐	☐

	Good	Average	Poor
Kitchen	☐	☐	☐
Cabinets	☐	☐	☐
Countertop	☐	☐	☐
Counter Space	☐	☐	☐
Flooring	☐	☐	☐
Oven / Stove	☐	☐	☐
Microwave	☐	☐	☐
Layout	☐	☐	☐
Light Fixtures	☐	☐	☐
Backsplash	☐	☐	☐
Pantry	☐	☐	☐
Appliances	☐	☐	☐
Island	☐	☐	☐

	Good	Average	Poor
Basement	☐	☐	☐
Garage	☐	☐	☐

COMMUNITY

	Good	Average	Poor
Immediate Neighborhood	☐	☐	☐
Close to Employment	☐	☐	☐
Close to Shopping	☐	☐	☐
Close to Transportation	☐	☐	☐
Close to Schools / Daycare	☐	☐	☐
Close to Places of Worship	☐	☐	☐
Near Recreational Facilities	☐	☐	☐
Close to Airport	☐	☐	☐
Near Police and Fire Department	☐	☐	☐

Address _____   Price _____

Bedrooms _____   Bathrooms _____   Sq.Ft. _____

Lot Size: _____   Year Built _____   School District _____

Annual Tax _____

EXTERIOR

	Good	Average	Poor
View/Yard/Landscaping	☐	☐	☐
Trees	☐	☐	☐
Lawn (Front)	☐	☐	☐
Lawn (Back)	☐	☐	☐
Fences (condition)	☐	☐	☐
Landscaping (condition)	☐	☐	☐
Irrigation / Sprinkler	☐	☐	☐
	☐	☐	☐
House Type	☐	☐	☐
Exterior Siding	☐	☐	☐
Deck / Patio / Porch	☐	☐	☐
Garage	☐	☐	☐
Window / Doors	☐	☐	☐
Roof / Gutters	☐	☐	☐
Fencing	☐	☐	☐

HOME SYSTEMS

	Good	Average	Poor
Electrical	☐	☐	☐
Air Conditioning / Fans	☐	☐	☐
Heating	☐	☐	☐
Security	☐	☐	☐
Plumbing	☐	☐	☐
Intercom	☐	☐	☐

FEATURES

	Good	Average	Poor
Home Warranty	☐	☐	☐
Energy Saving Features	☐	☐	☐

INTERIOR

	Good	Average	Poor
Walls / Trim / Ceilings	☐	☐	☐
Flooring	☐	☐	☐
Stairs	☐	☐	☐
Storage	☐	☐	☐
Living Room	☐	☐	☐
Family Room	☐	☐	☐
Dining Room	☐	☐	☐

	Good	Average	Poor
Master Bedroom	☐	☐	☐
Bedroom 2	☐	☐	☐
Bedroom 3	☐	☐	☐
Bedroom 4	☐	☐	☐
Master Bathroom	☐	☐	☐
Bathroom 2	☐	☐	☐
Bathroom 3	☐	☐	☐
Bonus / Game Room	☐	☐	☐

	Good	Average	Poor
Kitchen	☐	☐	☐
Cabinets	☐	☐	☐
Countertop	☐	☐	☐
Counter Space	☐	☐	☐
Flooring	☐	☐	☐
Oven / Stove	☐	☐	☐
Microwave	☐	☐	☐
Layout	☐	☐	☐
Light Fixtures	☐	☐	☐
Backsplash	☐	☐	☐
Pantry	☐	☐	☐
Appliances	☐	☐	☐
Island	☐	☐	☐

	Good	Average	Poor
Basement	☐	☐	☐
Garage	☐	☐	☐

COMMUNITY

	Good	Average	Poor
Immediate Neighborhood	☐	☐	☐
Close to Employment	☐	☐	☐
Close to Shopping	☐	☐	☐
Close to Transportation	☐	☐	☐
Close to Schools / Daycare	☐	☐	☐
Close to Places of Worship	☐	☐	☐
Near Recreational Facilities	☐	☐	☐
Close to Airport	☐	☐	☐
Near Police and Fire Department	☐	☐	☐

50

Address _____   Price _____

Bedrooms _____   Bathrooms _____   Sq.Ft. _____

Lot Size: _____   Year Built _____   School District _____

Annual Tax _____

EXTERIOR

	Good	Average	Poor
View/Yard/Landscaping	☐	☐	☐
Trees	☐	☐	☐
Lawn (Front)	☐	☐	☐
Lawn (Back)	☐	☐	☐
Fences (condition)	☐	☐	☐
Landscaping (condition)	☐	☐	☐
Irrigation / Sprinkler	☐	☐	☐
	☐	☐	☐
House Type	☐	☐	☐
Exterior Siding	☐	☐	☐
Deck / Patio / Porch	☐	☐	☐
Garage	☐	☐	☐
Window / Doors	☐	☐	☐
Roof / Gutters	☐	☐	☐
Fencing	☐	☐	☐

HOME SYSTEMS

	Good	Average	Poor
Electrical	☐	☐	☐
Air Conditioning / Fans	☐	☐	☐
Heating	☐	☐	☐
Security	☐	☐	☐
Plumbing	☐	☐	☐
Intercom	☐	☐	☐

FEATURES

	Good	Average	Poor
Home Warranty	☐	☐	☐
Energy Saving Features	☐	☐	☐

INTERIOR

	Good	Average	Poor
Walls / Trim / Ceilings	☐	☐	☐
Flooring	☐	☐	☐
Stairs	☐	☐	☐
Storage	☐	☐	☐
Living Room	☐	☐	☐
Family Room	☐	☐	☐
Dining Room	☐	☐	☐

	Good	Average	Poor
Master Bedroom	☐	☐	☐
Bedroom 2	☐	☐	☐
Bedroom 3	☐	☐	☐
Bedroom 4	☐	☐	☐
Master Bathroom	☐	☐	☐
Bathroom 2	☐	☐	☐
Bathroom 3	☐	☐	☐
Bonus / Game Room	☐	☐	☐

	Good	Average	Poor
Kitchen	☐	☐	☐
Cabinets	☐	☐	☐
Countertop	☐	☐	☐
Counter Space	☐	☐	☐
Flooring	☐	☐	☐
Oven / Stove	☐	☐	☐
Microwave	☐	☐	☐
Layout	☐	☐	☐
Light Fixtures	☐	☐	☐
Backsplash	☐	☐	☐
Pantry	☐	☐	☐
Appliances	☐	☐	☐
Island	☐	☐	☐

	Good	Average	Poor
Basement	☐	☐	☐
Garage	☐	☐	☐

COMMUNITY

	Good	Average	Poor
Immediate Neighborhood	☐	☐	☐
Close to Employment	☐	☐	☐
Close to Shopping	☐	☐	☐
Close to Transportation	☐	☐	☐
Close to Schools / Daycare	☐	☐	☐
Close to Places of Worship	☐	☐	☐
Near Recreational Facilities	☐	☐	☐
Close to Airport	☐	☐	☐
Near Police and Fire Department	☐	☐	☐

Address _____   Price _____

Bedrooms _____   Bathrooms _____   Sq.Ft. _____

Lot Size: _____   Year Built _____   School District _____

Annual Tax _____

EXTERIOR

	Good	Average	Poor
View/Yard/Landscaping	☐	☐	☐
Trees	☐	☐	☐
Lawn (Front)	☐	☐	☐
Lawn (Back)	☐	☐	☐
Fences (condition)	☐	☐	☐
Landscaping (condition)	☐	☐	☐
Irrigation / Sprinkler	☐	☐	☐
	☐	☐	☐
House Type	☐	☐	☐
Exterior Siding	☐	☐	☐
Deck / Patio / Porch	☐	☐	☐
Garage	☐	☐	☐
Window / Doors	☐	☐	☐
Roof / Gutters	☐	☐	☐
Fencing	☐	☐	☐

HOME SYSTEMS

	Good	Average	Poor
Electrical	☐	☐	☐
Air Conditioning / Fans	☐	☐	☐
Heating	☐	☐	☐
Security	☐	☐	☐
Plumbing	☐	☐	☐
Intercom	☐	☐	☐

FEATURES

	Good	Average	Poor
Home Warranty	☐	☐	☐
Energy Saving Features	☐	☐	☐

INTERIOR

	Good	Average	Poor
Walls / Trim / Ceilings	☐	☐	☐
Flooring	☐	☐	☐
Stairs	☐	☐	☐
Storage	☐	☐	☐
Living Room	☐	☐	☐
Family Room	☐	☐	☐
Dining Room	☐	☐	☐

	Good	Average	Poor
Master Bedroom	☐	☐	☐
Bedroom 2	☐	☐	☐
Bedroom 3	☐	☐	☐
Bedroom 4	☐	☐	☐
Master Bathroom	☐	☐	☐
Bathroom 2	☐	☐	☐
Bathroom 3	☐	☐	☐
Bonus / Game Room	☐	☐	☐

	Good	Average	Poor
Kitchen	☐	☐	☐
Cabinets	☐	☐	☐
Countertop	☐	☐	☐
Counter Space	☐	☐	☐
Flooring	☐	☐	☐
Oven / Stove	☐	☐	☐
Microwave	☐	☐	☐
Layout	☐	☐	☐
Light Fixtures	☐	☐	☐
Backsplash	☐	☐	☐
Pantry	☐	☐	☐
Appliances	☐	☐	☐
Island	☐	☐	☐

	Good	Average	Poor
Basement	☐	☐	☐
Garage	☐	☐	☐

COMMUNITY

	Good	Average	Poor
Immediate Neighborhood	☐	☐	☐
Close to Employment	☐	☐	☐
Close to Shopping	☐	☐	☐
Close to Transportation	☐	☐	☐
Close to Schools / Daycare	☐	☐	☐
Close to Places of Worship	☐	☐	☐
Near Recreational Facilities	☐	☐	☐
Close to Airport	☐	☐	☐
Near Police and Fire Department	☐	☐	☐

Address _____   Price _____

Bedrooms _____   Bathrooms _____   Sq.Ft. _____

Lot Size: _____   Year Built _____   School District _____

Annual Tax _____

EXTERIOR

	Good	Average	Poor
View/Yard/Landscaping	☐	☐	☐
Trees	☐	☐	☐
Lawn (Front)	☐	☐	☐
Lawn (Back)	☐	☐	☐
Fences (condition)	☐	☐	☐
Landscaping (condition)	☐	☐	☐
Irrigation / Sprinkler	☐	☐	☐
	☐	☐	☐
House Type	☐	☐	☐
Exterior Siding	☐	☐	☐
Deck / Patio / Porch	☐	☐	☐
Garage	☐	☐	☐
Window / Doors	☐	☐	☐
Roof / Gutters	☐	☐	☐
Fencing	☐	☐	☐

HOME SYSTEMS

	Good	Average	Poor
Electrical	☐	☐	☐
Air Conditioning / Fans	☐	☐	☐
Heating	☐	☐	☐
Security	☐	☐	☐
Plumbing	☐	☐	☐
Intercom	☐	☐	☐

FEATURES

	Good	Average	Poor
Home Warranty	☐	☐	☐
Energy Saving Features	☐	☐	☐

INTERIOR

	Good	Average	Poor
Walls / Trim / Ceilings	☐	☐	☐
Flooring	☐	☐	☐
Stairs	☐	☐	☐
Storage	☐	☐	☐
Living Room	☐	☐	☐
Family Room	☐	☐	☐
Dining Room	☐	☐	☐

	Good	Average	Poor
Master Bedroom	☐	☐	☐
Bedroom 2	☐	☐	☐
Bedroom 3	☐	☐	☐
Bedroom 4	☐	☐	☐
Master Bathroom	☐	☐	☐
Bathroom 2	☐	☐	☐
Bathroom 3	☐	☐	☐
Bonus / Game Room	☐	☐	☐

	Good	Average	Poor
Kitchen	☐	☐	☐
Cabinets	☐	☐	☐
Countertop	☐	☐	☐
Counter Space	☐	☐	☐
Flooring	☐	☐	☐
Oven / Stove	☐	☐	☐
Microwave	☐	☐	☐
Layout	☐	☐	☐
Light Fixtures	☐	☐	☐
Backsplash	☐	☐	☐
Pantry	☐	☐	☐
Appliances	☐	☐	☐
Island	☐	☐	☐

	Good	Average	Poor
Basement	☐	☐	☐
Garage	☐	☐	☐

COMMUNITY

	Good	Average	Poor
Immediate Neighborhood	☐	☐	☐
Close to Employment	☐	☐	☐
Close to Shopping	☐	☐	☐
Close to Transportation	☐	☐	☐
Close to Schools / Daycare	☐	☐	☐
Close to Places of Worship	☐	☐	☐
Near Recreational Facilities	☐	☐	☐
Close to Airport	☐	☐	☐
Near Police and Fire Department	☐	☐	☐

Address _____   Price _____

Bedrooms _____   Bathrooms _____   Sq.Ft. _____

Lot Size: _____   Year Built _____   School District _____

Annual Tax _____

EXTERIOR

	Good	Average	Poor
View/Yard/Landscaping	☐	☐	☐
Trees	☐	☐	☐
Lawn (Front)	☐	☐	☐
Lawn (Back)	☐	☐	☐
Fences (condition)	☐	☐	☐
Landscaping (condition)	☐	☐	☐
Irrigation / Sprinkler	☐	☐	☐
	☐	☐	☐
House Type	☐	☐	☐
Exterior Siding	☐	☐	☐
Deck / Patio / Porch	☐	☐	☐
Garage	☐	☐	☐
Window / Doors	☐	☐	☐
Roof / Gutters	☐	☐	☐
Fencing	☐	☐	☐

HOME SYSTEMS

	Good	Average	Poor
Electrical	☐	☐	☐
Air Conditioning / Fans	☐	☐	☐
Heating	☐	☐	☐
Security	☐	☐	☐
Plumbing	☐	☐	☐
Intercom	☐	☐	☐

FEATURES

	Good	Average	Poor
Home Warranty	☐	☐	☐
Energy Saving Features	☐	☐	☐

INTERIOR

	Good	Average	Poor
Walls / Trim / Ceilings	☐	☐	☐
Flooring	☐	☐	☐
Stairs	☐	☐	☐
Storage	☐	☐	☐
Living Room	☐	☐	☐
Family Room	☐	☐	☐
Dining Room	☐	☐	☐

	Good	Average	Poor
Master Bedroom	☐	☐	☐
Bedroom 2	☐	☐	☐
Bedroom 3	☐	☐	☐
Bedroom 4	☐	☐	☐
Master Bathroom	☐	☐	☐
Bathroom 2	☐	☐	☐
Bathroom 3	☐	☐	☐
Bonus / Game Room	☐	☐	☐

	Good	Average	Poor
Kitchen	☐	☐	☐
Cabinets	☐	☐	☐
Countertop	☐	☐	☐
Counter Space	☐	☐	☐
Flooring	☐	☐	☐
Oven / Stove	☐	☐	☐
Microwave	☐	☐	☐
Layout	☐	☐	☐
Light Fixtures	☐	☐	☐
Backsplash	☐	☐	☐
Pantry	☐	☐	☐
Appliances	☐	☐	☐
Island	☐	☐	☐

	Good	Average	Poor
Basement	☐	☐	☐
Garage	☐	☐	☐

COMMUNITY

	Good	Average	Poor
Immediate Neighborhood	☐	☐	☐
Close to Employment	☐	☐	☐
Close to Shopping	☐	☐	☐
Close to Transportation	☐	☐	☐
Close to Schools / Daycare	☐	☐	☐
Close to Places of Worship	☐	☐	☐
Near Recreational Facilities	☐	☐	☐
Close to Airport	☐	☐	☐
Near Police and Fire Department	☐	☐	☐

54

Address _____ Price _____

Bedrooms _____ Bathrooms _____ Sq.Ft. _____

Lot Size: _____ Year Built _____ School District _____

Annual Tax _____

EXTERIOR

	Good	Average	Poor
View/Yard/Landscaping	☐	☐	☐
Trees	☐	☐	☐
Lawn (Front)	☐	☐	☐
Lawn (Back)	☐	☐	☐
Fences (condition)	☐	☐	☐
Landscaping (condition)	☐	☐	☐
Irrigation / Sprinkler	☐	☐	☐
	☐	☐	☐
House Type	☐	☐	☐
Exterior Siding	☐	☐	☐
Deck / Patio / Porch	☐	☐	☐
Garage	☐	☐	☐
Window / Doors	☐	☐	☐
Roof / Gutters	☐	☐	☐
Fencing	☐	☐	☐

HOME SYSTEMS

	Good	Average	Poor
Electrical	☐	☐	☐
Air Conditioning / Fans	☐	☐	☐
Heating	☐	☐	☐
Security	☐	☐	☐
Plumbing	☐	☐	☐
Intercom	☐	☐	☐

FEATURES

	Good	Average	Poor
Home Warranty	☐	☐	☐
Energy Saving Features	☐	☐	☐

INTERIOR

	Good	Average	Poor
Walls / Trim / Ceilings	☐	☐	☐
Flooring	☐	☐	☐
Stairs	☐	☐	☐
Storage	☐	☐	☐
Living Room	☐	☐	☐
Family Room	☐	☐	☐
Dining Room	☐	☐	☐

	Good	Average	Poor
Master Bedroom	☐	☐	☐
Bedroom 2	☐	☐	☐
Bedroom 3	☐	☐	☐
Bedroom 4	☐	☐	☐
Master Bathroom	☐	☐	☐
Bathroom 2	☐	☐	☐
Bathroom 3	☐	☐	☐
Bonus / Game Room	☐	☐	☐

	Good	Average	Poor
Kitchen	☐	☐	☐
Cabinets	☐	☐	☐
Countertop	☐	☐	☐
Counter Space	☐	☐	☐
Flooring	☐	☐	☐
Oven / Stove	☐	☐	☐
Microwave	☐	☐	☐
Layout	☐	☐	☐
Light Fixtures	☐	☐	☐
Backsplash	☐	☐	☐
Pantry	☐	☐	☐
Appliances	☐	☐	☐
Island	☐	☐	☐

	Good	Average	Poor
Basement	☐	☐	☐
Garage	☐	☐	☐

COMMUNITY

	Good	Average	Poor
Immediate Neighborhood	☐	☐	☐
Close to Employment	☐	☐	☐
Close to Shopping	☐	☐	☐
Close to Transportation	☐	☐	☐
Close to Schools / Daycare	☐	☐	☐
Close to Places of Worship	☐	☐	☐
Near Recreational Facilities	☐	☐	☐
Close to Airport	☐	☐	☐
Near Police and Fire Department	☐	☐	☐

Address _____   Price _____

Bedrooms _____   Bathrooms _____   Sq.Ft. _____

Lot Size: _____   Year Built _____   School District _____

Annual Tax _____

EXTERIOR

	Good	Average	Poor
View/Yard/Landscaping	☐	☐	☐
Trees	☐	☐	☐
Lawn (Front)	☐	☐	☐
Lawn (Back)	☐	☐	☐
Fences (condition)	☐	☐	☐
Landscaping (condition)	☐	☐	☐
Irrigation / Sprinkler	☐	☐	☐
	☐	☐	☐
House Type	☐	☐	☐
Exterior Siding	☐	☐	☐
Deck / Patio / Porch	☐	☐	☐
Garage	☐	☐	☐
Window / Doors	☐	☐	☐
Roof / Gutters	☐	☐	☐
Fencing	☐	☐	☐

HOME SYSTEMS

	Good	Average	Poor
Electrical	☐	☐	☐
Air Conditioning / Fans	☐	☐	☐
Heating	☐	☐	☐
Security	☐	☐	☐
Plumbing	☐	☐	☐
Intercom	☐	☐	☐

FEATURES

	Good	Average	Poor
Home Warranty	☐	☐	☐
Energy Saving Features	☐	☐	☐

INTERIOR

	Good	Average	Poor
Walls / Trim / Ceilings	☐	☐	☐
Flooring	☐	☐	☐
Stairs	☐	☐	☐
Storage	☐	☐	☐
Living Room	☐	☐	☐
Family Room	☐	☐	☐
Dining Room	☐	☐	☐

	Good	Average	Poor
Master Bedroom	☐	☐	☐
Bedroom 2	☐	☐	☐
Bedroom 3	☐	☐	☐
Bedroom 4	☐	☐	☐
Master Bathroom	☐	☐	☐
Bathroom 2	☐	☐	☐
Bathroom 3	☐	☐	☐
Bonus / Game Room	☐	☐	☐

	Good	Average	Poor
Kitchen	☐	☐	☐
Cabinets	☐	☐	☐
Countertop	☐	☐	☐
Counter Space	☐	☐	☐
Flooring	☐	☐	☐
Oven / Stove	☐	☐	☐
Microwave	☐	☐	☐
Layout	☐	☐	☐
Light Fixtures	☐	☐	☐
Backsplash	☐	☐	☐
Pantry	☐	☐	☐
Appliances	☐	☐	☐
Island	☐	☐	☐

	Good	Average	Poor
Basement	☐	☐	☐
Garage	☐	☐	☐

COMMUNITY

	Good	Average	Poor
Immediate Neighborhood	☐	☐	☐
Close to Employment	☐	☐	☐
Close to Shopping	☐	☐	☐
Close to Transportation	☐	☐	☐
Close to Schools / Daycare	☐	☐	☐
Close to Places of Worship	☐	☐	☐
Near Recreational Facilities	☐	☐	☐
Close to Airport	☐	☐	☐
Near Police and Fire Department	☐	☐	☐

Address _____   Price _____

Bedrooms _____   Bathrooms _____   Sq.Ft. _____

Lot Size: _____   Year Built _____   School District _____

Annual Tax _____

EXTERIOR

	Good	Average	Poor
View/Yard/Landscaping	☐	☐	☐
Trees	☐	☐	☐
Lawn (Front)	☐	☐	☐
Lawn (Back)	☐	☐	☐
Fences (condition)	☐	☐	☐
Landscaping (condition)	☐	☐	☐
Irrigation / Sprinkler	☐	☐	☐
	☐	☐	☐
House Type	☐	☐	☐
Exterior Siding	☐	☐	☐
Deck / Patio / Porch	☐	☐	☐
Garage	☐	☐	☐
Window / Doors	☐	☐	☐
Roof / Gutters	☐	☐	☐
Fencing	☐	☐	☐

HOME SYSTEMS

	Good	Average	Poor
Electrical	☐	☐	☐
Air Conditioning / Fans	☐	☐	☐
Heating	☐	☐	☐
Security	☐	☐	☐
Plumbing	☐	☐	☐
Intercom	☐	☐	☐

FEATURES

	Good	Average	Poor
Home Warranty	☐	☐	☐
Energy Saving Features	☐	☐	☐

INTERIOR

	Good	Average	Poor
Walls / Trim / Ceilings	☐	☐	☐
Flooring	☐	☐	☐
Stairs	☐	☐	☐
Storage	☐	☐	☐
Living Room	☐	☐	☐
Family Room	☐	☐	☐
Dining Room	☐	☐	☐

	Good	Average	Poor
Master Bedroom	☐	☐	☐
Bedroom 2	☐	☐	☐
Bedroom 3	☐	☐	☐
Bedroom 4	☐	☐	☐
Master Bathroom	☐	☐	☐
Bathroom 2	☐	☐	☐
Bathroom 3	☐	☐	☐
Bonus / Game Room	☐	☐	☐

	Good	Average	Poor
Kitchen	☐	☐	☐
Cabinets	☐	☐	☐
Countertop	☐	☐	☐
Counter Space	☐	☐	☐
Flooring	☐	☐	☐
Oven / Stove	☐	☐	☐
Microwave	☐	☐	☐
Layout	☐	☐	☐
Light Fixtures	☐	☐	☐
Backsplash	☐	☐	☐
Pantry	☐	☐	☐
Appliances	☐	☐	☐
Island	☐	☐	☐

	Good	Average	Poor
Basement	☐	☐	☐
Garage	☐	☐	☐

COMMUNITY

	Good	Average	Poor
Immediate Neighborhood	☐	☐	☐
Close to Employment	☐	☐	☐
Close to Shopping	☐	☐	☐
Close to Transportation	☐	☐	☐
Close to Schools / Daycare	☐	☐	☐
Close to Places of Worship	☐	☐	☐
Near Recreational Facilities	☐	☐	☐
Close to Airport	☐	☐	☐
Near Police and Fire Department	☐	☐	☐

Address _____   Price _____

Bedrooms _____   Bathrooms _____   Sq.Ft. _____

Lot Size: _____   Year Built _____   School District _____

Annual Tax _____

EXTERIOR

	Good	Average	Poor
View/Yard/Landscaping	☐	☐	☐
Trees	☐	☐	☐
Lawn (Front)	☐	☐	☐
Lawn (Back)	☐	☐	☐
Fences (condition)	☐	☐	☐
Landscaping (condition)	☐	☐	☐
Irrigation / Sprinkler	☐	☐	☐
	☐	☐	☐
House Type	☐	☐	☐
Exterior Siding	☐	☐	☐
Deck / Patio / Porch	☐	☐	☐
Garage	☐	☐	☐
Window / Doors	☐	☐	☐
Roof / Gutters	☐	☐	☐
Fencing	☐	☐	☐

HOME SYSTEMS

	Good	Average	Poor
Electrical	☐	☐	☐
Air Conditioning / Fans	☐	☐	☐
Heating	☐	☐	☐
Security	☐	☐	☐
Plumbing	☐	☐	☐
Intercom	☐	☐	☐

FEATURES

	Good	Average	Poor
Home Warranty	☐	☐	☐
Energy Saving Features	☐	☐	☐

INTERIOR

	Good	Average	Poor
Walls / Trim / Ceilings	☐	☐	☐
Flooring	☐	☐	☐
Stairs	☐	☐	☐
Storage	☐	☐	☐
Living Room	☐	☐	☐
Family Room	☐	☐	☐
Dining Room	☐	☐	☐

	Good	Average	Poor
Master Bedroom	☐	☐	☐
Bedroom 2	☐	☐	☐
Bedroom 3	☐	☐	☐
Bedroom 4	☐	☐	☐
Master Bathroom	☐	☐	☐
Bathroom 2	☐	☐	☐
Bathroom 3	☐	☐	☐
Bonus / Game Room	☐	☐	☐

	Good	Average	Poor
Kitchen	☐	☐	☐
Cabinets	☐	☐	☐
Countertop	☐	☐	☐
Counter Space	☐	☐	☐
Flooring	☐	☐	☐
Oven / Stove	☐	☐	☐
Microwave	☐	☐	☐
Layout	☐	☐	☐
Light Fixtures	☐	☐	☐
Backsplash	☐	☐	☐
Pantry	☐	☐	☐
Appliances	☐	☐	☐
Island	☐	☐	☐

	Good	Average	Poor
Basement	☐	☐	☐
Garage	☐	☐	☐

COMMUNITY

	Good	Average	Poor
Immediate Neighborhood	☐	☐	☐
Close to Employment	☐	☐	☐
Close to Shopping	☐	☐	☐
Close to Transportation	☐	☐	☐
Close to Schools / Daycare	☐	☐	☐
Close to Places of Worship	☐	☐	☐
Near Recreational Facilities	☐	☐	☐
Close to Airport	☐	☐	☐
Near Police and Fire Department	☐	☐	☐

Address _____ Price _____

Bedrooms _____ Bathrooms _____ Sq.Ft. _____

Lot Size: _____ Year Built _____ School District _____

Annual Tax _____

EXTERIOR

	Good	Average	Poor
View/Yard/Landscaping	☐	☐	☐
Trees	☐	☐	☐
Lawn (Front)	☐	☐	☐
Lawn (Back)	☐	☐	☐
Fences (condition)	☐	☐	☐
Landscaping (condition)	☐	☐	☐
Irrigation / Sprinkler	☐	☐	☐
	☐	☐	☐
House Type	☐	☐	☐
Exterior Siding	☐	☐	☐
Deck / Patio / Porch	☐	☐	☐
Garage	☐	☐	☐
Window / Doors	☐	☐	☐
Roof / Gutters	☐	☐	☐
Fencing	☐	☐	☐

HOME SYSTEMS

	Good	Average	Poor
Electrical	☐	☐	☐
Air Conditioning / Fans	☐	☐	☐
Heating	☐	☐	☐
Security	☐	☐	☐
Plumbing	☐	☐	☐
Intercom	☐	☐	☐

FEATURES

	Good	Average	Poor
Home Warranty	☐	☐	☐
Energy Saving Features	☐	☐	☐

INTERIOR

	Good	Average	Poor
Walls / Trim / Ceilings	☐	☐	☐
Flooring	☐	☐	☐
Stairs	☐	☐	☐
Storage	☐	☐	☐
Living Room	☐	☐	☐
Family Room	☐	☐	☐
Dining Room	☐	☐	☐

	Good	Average	Poor
Master Bedroom	☐	☐	☐
Bedroom 2	☐	☐	☐
Bedroom 3	☐	☐	☐
Bedroom 4	☐	☐	☐
Master Bathroom	☐	☐	☐
Bathroom 2	☐	☐	☐
Bathroom 3	☐	☐	☐
Bonus / Game Room	☐	☐	☐

	Good	Average	Poor
Kitchen	☐	☐	☐
Cabinets	☐	☐	☐
Countertop	☐	☐	☐
Counter Space	☐	☐	☐
Flooring	☐	☐	☐
Oven / Stove	☐	☐	☐
Microwave	☐	☐	☐
Layout	☐	☐	☐
Light Fixtures	☐	☐	☐
Backsplash	☐	☐	☐
Pantry	☐	☐	☐
Appliances	☐	☐	☐
Island	☐	☐	☐

	Good	Average	Poor
Basement	☐	☐	☐
Garage	☐	☐	☐

COMMUNITY

	Good	Average	Poor
Immediate Neighborhood	☐	☐	☐
Close to Employment	☐	☐	☐
Close to Shopping	☐	☐	☐
Close to Transportation	☐	☐	☐
Close to Schools / Daycare	☐	☐	☐
Close to Places of Worship	☐	☐	☐
Near Recreational Facilities	☐	☐	☐
Close to Airport	☐	☐	☐
Near Police and Fire Department	☐	☐	☐

59

Address _____   Price _____

Bedrooms _____   Bathrooms _____   Sq.Ft. _____

Lot Size: _____   Year Built _____   School District _____

Annual Tax _____

EXTERIOR

	Good	Average	Poor
View/Yard/Landscaping	☐	☐	☐
Trees	☐	☐	☐
Lawn (Front)	☐	☐	☐
Lawn (Back)	☐	☐	☐
Fences (condition)	☐	☐	☐
Landscaping (condition)	☐	☐	☐
Irrigation / Sprinkler	☐	☐	☐
	☐	☐	☐
House Type	☐	☐	☐
Exterior Siding	☐	☐	☐
Deck / Patio / Porch	☐	☐	☐
Garage	☐	☐	☐
Window / Doors	☐	☐	☐
Roof / Gutters	☐	☐	☐
Fencing	☐	☐	☐

HOME SYSTEMS

	Good	Average	Poor
Electrical	☐	☐	☐
Air Conditioning / Fans	☐	☐	☐
Heating	☐	☐	☐
Security	☐	☐	☐
Plumbing	☐	☐	☐
Intercom	☐	☐	☐

FEATURES

	Good	Average	Poor
Home Warranty	☐	☐	☐
Energy Saving Features	☐	☐	☐

INTERIOR

	Good	Average	Poor
Walls / Trim / Ceilings	☐	☐	☐
Flooring	☐	☐	☐
Stairs	☐	☐	☐
Storage	☐	☐	☐
Living Room	☐	☐	☐
Family Room	☐	☐	☐
Dining Room	☐	☐	☐

	Good	Average	Poor
Master Bedroom	☐	☐	☐
Bedroom 2	☐	☐	☐
Bedroom 3	☐	☐	☐
Bedroom 4	☐	☐	☐
Master Bathroom	☐	☐	☐
Bathroom 2	☐	☐	☐
Bathroom 3	☐	☐	☐
Bonus / Game Room	☐	☐	☐

	Good	Average	Poor
Kitchen	☐	☐	☐
Cabinets	☐	☐	☐
Countertop	☐	☐	☐
Counter Space	☐	☐	☐
Flooring	☐	☐	☐
Oven / Stove	☐	☐	☐
Microwave	☐	☐	☐
Layout	☐	☐	☐
Light Fixtures	☐	☐	☐
Backsplash	☐	☐	☐
Pantry	☐	☐	☐
Appliances	☐	☐	☐
Island	☐	☐	☐

	Good	Average	Poor
Basement	☐	☐	☐
Garage	☐	☐	☐

COMMUNITY

	Good	Average	Poor
Immediate Neighborhood	☐	☐	☐
Close to Employment	☐	☐	☐
Close to Shopping	☐	☐	☐
Close to Transportation	☐	☐	☐
Close to Schools / Daycare	☐	☐	☐
Close to Places of Worship	☐	☐	☐
Near Recreational Facilities	☐	☐	☐
Close to Airport	☐	☐	☐
Near Police and Fire Department	☐	☐	☐

60

Address _____ Price _____

Bedrooms _____ Bathrooms _____ Sq.Ft. _____

Lot Size: _____ Year Built _____ School District _____

Annual Tax _____

EXTERIOR

	Good	Average	Poor
View/Yard/Landscaping	☐	☐	☐
Trees	☐	☐	☐
Lawn (Front)	☐	☐	☐
Lawn (Back)	☐	☐	☐
Fences (condition)	☐	☐	☐
Landscaping (condition)	☐	☐	☐
Irrigation / Sprinkler	☐	☐	☐
	☐	☐	☐
House Type	☐	☐	☐
Exterior Siding	☐	☐	☐
Deck / Patio / Porch	☐	☐	☐
Garage	☐	☐	☐
Window / Doors	☐	☐	☐
Roof / Gutters	☐	☐	☐
Fencing	☐	☐	☐

HOME SYSTEMS

	Good	Average	Poor
Electrical	☐	☐	☐
Air Conditioning / Fans	☐	☐	☐
Heating	☐	☐	☐
Security	☐	☐	☐
Plumbing	☐	☐	☐
Intercom	☐	☐	☐

FEATURES

	Good	Average	Poor
Home Warranty	☐	☐	☐
Energy Saving Features	☐	☐	☐

INTERIOR

	Good	Average	Poor
Walls / Trim / Ceilings	☐	☐	☐
Flooring	☐	☐	☐
Stairs	☐	☐	☐
Storage	☐	☐	☐
Living Room	☐	☐	☐
Family Room	☐	☐	☐
Dining Room	☐	☐	☐

	Good	Average	Poor
Master Bedroom	☐	☐	☐
Bedroom 2	☐	☐	☐
Bedroom 3	☐	☐	☐
Bedroom 4	☐	☐	☐
Master Bathroom	☐	☐	☐
Bathroom 2	☐	☐	☐
Bathroom 3	☐	☐	☐
Bonus / Game Room	☐	☐	☐

	Good	Average	Poor
Kitchen	☐	☐	☐
Cabinets	☐	☐	☐
Countertop	☐	☐	☐
Counter Space	☐	☐	☐
Flooring	☐	☐	☐
Oven / Stove	☐	☐	☐
Microwave	☐	☐	☐
Layout	☐	☐	☐
Light Fixtures	☐	☐	☐
Backsplash	☐	☐	☐
Pantry	☐	☐	☐
Appliances	☐	☐	☐
Island	☐	☐	☐

	Good	Average	Poor
Basement	☐	☐	☐
Garage	☐	☐	☐

COMMUNITY

	Good	Average	Poor
Immediate Neighborhood	☐	☐	☐
Close to Employment	☐	☐	☐
Close to Shopping	☐	☐	☐
Close to Transportation	☐	☐	☐
Close to Schools / Daycare	☐	☐	☐
Close to Places of Worship	☐	☐	☐
Near Recreational Facilities	☐	☐	☐
Close to Airport	☐	☐	☐
Near Police and Fire Department	☐	☐	☐

Address _____   Price _____

Bedrooms _____   Bathrooms _____   Sq.Ft. _____

Lot Size: _____   Year Built _____   School District _____

Annual Tax _____

EXTERIOR

	Good	Average	Poor
View/Yard/Landscaping	☐	☐	☐
Trees	☐	☐	☐
Lawn (Front)	☐	☐	☐
Lawn (Back)	☐	☐	☐
Fences (condition)	☐	☐	☐
Landscaping (condition)	☐	☐	☐
Irrigation / Sprinkler	☐	☐	☐
	☐	☐	☐
House Type	☐	☐	☐
Exterior Siding	☐	☐	☐
Deck / Patio / Porch	☐	☐	☐
Garage	☐	☐	☐
Window / Doors	☐	☐	☐
Roof / Gutters	☐	☐	☐
Fencing	☐	☐	☐

HOME SYSTEMS

	Good	Average	Poor
Electrical	☐	☐	☐
Air Conditioning / Fans	☐	☐	☐
Heating	☐	☐	☐
Security	☐	☐	☐
Plumbing	☐	☐	☐
Intercom	☐	☐	☐

FEATURES

	Good	Average	Poor
Home Warranty	☐	☐	☐
Energy Saving Features	☐	☐	☐

INTERIOR

	Good	Average	Poor
Walls / Trim / Ceilings	☐	☐	☐
Flooring	☐	☐	☐
Stairs	☐	☐	☐
Storage	☐	☐	☐
Living Room	☐	☐	☐
Family Room	☐	☐	☐
Dining Room	☐	☐	☐

	Good	Average	Poor
Master Bedroom	☐	☐	☐
Bedroom 2	☐	☐	☐
Bedroom 3	☐	☐	☐
Bedroom 4	☐	☐	☐
Master Bathroom	☐	☐	☐
Bathroom 2	☐	☐	☐
Bathroom 3	☐	☐	☐
Bonus / Game Room	☐	☐	☐

	Good	Average	Poor
Kitchen	☐	☐	☐
Cabinets	☐	☐	☐
Countertop	☐	☐	☐
Counter Space	☐	☐	☐
Flooring	☐	☐	☐
Oven / Stove	☐	☐	☐
Microwave	☐	☐	☐
Layout	☐	☐	☐
Light Fixtures	☐	☐	☐
Backsplash	☐	☐	☐
Pantry	☐	☐	☐
Appliances	☐	☐	☐
Island	☐	☐	☐

	Good	Average	Poor
Basement	☐	☐	☐
Garage	☐	☐	☐

COMMUNITY

	Good	Average	Poor
Immediate Neighborhood	☐	☐	☐
Close to Employment	☐	☐	☐
Close to Shopping	☐	☐	☐
Close to Transportation	☐	☐	☐
Close to Schools / Daycare	☐	☐	☐
Close to Places of Worship	☐	☐	☐
Near Recreational Facilities	☐	☐	☐
Close to Airport	☐	☐	☐
Near Police and Fire Department	☐	☐	☐

Address _____   Price _____

Bedrooms _____   Bathrooms _____   Sq.Ft. _____

Lot Size: _____   Year Built _____   School District _____

Annual Tax _____

EXTERIOR

	Good	Average	Poor
View/Yard/Landscaping	☐	☐	☐
Trees	☐	☐	☐
Lawn (Front)	☐	☐	☐
Lawn (Back)	☐	☐	☐
Fences (condition)	☐	☐	☐
Landscaping (condition)	☐	☐	☐
Irrigation / Sprinkler	☐	☐	☐
	☐	☐	☐
House Type	☐	☐	☐
Exterior Siding	☐	☐	☐
Deck / Patio / Porch	☐	☐	☐
Garage	☐	☐	☐
Window / Doors	☐	☐	☐
Roof / Gutters	☐	☐	☐
Fencing	☐	☐	☐

HOME SYSTEMS

	Good	Average	Poor
Electrical	☐	☐	☐
Air Conditioning / Fans	☐	☐	☐
Heating	☐	☐	☐
Security	☐	☐	☐
Plumbing	☐	☐	☐
Intercom	☐	☐	☐

FEATURES

	Good	Average	Poor
Home Warranty	☐	☐	☐
Energy Saving Features	☐	☐	☐

INTERIOR

	Good	Average	Poor
Walls / Trim / Ceilings	☐	☐	☐
Flooring	☐	☐	☐
Stairs	☐	☐	☐
Storage	☐	☐	☐
Living Room	☐	☐	☐
Family Room	☐	☐	☐
Dining Room	☐	☐	☐

	Good	Average	Poor
Master Bedroom	☐	☐	☐
Bedroom 2	☐	☐	☐
Bedroom 3	☐	☐	☐
Bedroom 4	☐	☐	☐
Master Bathroom	☐	☐	☐
Bathroom 2	☐	☐	☐
Bathroom 3	☐	☐	☐
Bonus / Game Room	☐	☐	☐

	Good	Average	Poor
Kitchen	☐	☐	☐
Cabinets	☐	☐	☐
Countertop	☐	☐	☐
Counter Space	☐	☐	☐
Flooring	☐	☐	☐
Oven / Stove	☐	☐	☐
Microwave	☐	☐	☐
Layout	☐	☐	☐
Light Fixtures	☐	☐	☐
Backsplash	☐	☐	☐
Pantry	☐	☐	☐
Appliances	☐	☐	☐
Island	☐	☐	☐

	Good	Average	Poor
Basement	☐	☐	☐
Garage	☐	☐	☐

COMMUNITY

	Good	Average	Poor
Immediate Neighborhood	☐	☐	☐
Close to Employment	☐	☐	☐
Close to Shopping	☐	☐	☐
Close to Transportation	☐	☐	☐
Close to Schools / Daycare	☐	☐	☐
Close to Places of Worship	☐	☐	☐
Near Recreational Facilities	☐	☐	☐
Close to Airport	☐	☐	☐
Near Police and Fire Department	☐	☐	☐

63

Address _____ Price _____

Bedrooms _____ Bathrooms _____ Sq.Ft. _____

Lot Size: _____ Year Built _____ School District _____

Annual Tax _____

EXTERIOR

	Good	Average	Poor
View/Yard/Landscaping	☐	☐	☐
Trees	☐	☐	☐
Lawn (Front)	☐	☐	☐
Lawn (Back)	☐	☐	☐
Fences (condition)	☐	☐	☐
Landscaping (condition)	☐	☐	☐
Irrigation / Sprinkler	☐	☐	☐
	☐	☐	☐
House Type	☐	☐	☐
Exterior Siding	☐	☐	☐
Deck / Patio / Porch	☐	☐	☐
Garage	☐	☐	☐
Window / Doors	☐	☐	☐
Roof / Gutters	☐	☐	☐
Fencing	☐	☐	☐

HOME SYSTEMS

	Good	Average	Poor
Electrical	☐	☐	☐
Air Conditioning / Fans	☐	☐	☐
Heating	☐	☐	☐
Security	☐	☐	☐
Plumbing	☐	☐	☐
Intercom	☐	☐	☐

FEATURES

	Good	Average	Poor
Home Warranty	☐	☐	☐
Energy Saving Features	☐	☐	☐

INTERIOR

	Good	Average	Poor
Walls / Trim / Ceilings	☐	☐	☐
Flooring	☐	☐	☐
Stairs	☐	☐	☐
Storage	☐	☐	☐
Living Room	☐	☐	☐
Family Room	☐	☐	☐
Dining Room	☐	☐	☐

	Good	Average	Poor
Master Bedroom	☐	☐	☐
Bedroom 2	☐	☐	☐
Bedroom 3	☐	☐	☐
Bedroom 4	☐	☐	☐
Master Bathroom	☐	☐	☐
Bathroom 2	☐	☐	☐
Bathroom 3	☐	☐	☐
Bonus / Game Room	☐	☐	☐

	Good	Average	Poor
Kitchen	☐	☐	☐
Cabinets	☐	☐	☐
Countertop	☐	☐	☐
Counter Space	☐	☐	☐
Flooring	☐	☐	☐
Oven / Stove	☐	☐	☐
Microwave	☐	☐	☐
Layout	☐	☐	☐
Light Fixtures	☐	☐	☐
Backsplash	☐	☐	☐
Pantry	☐	☐	☐
Appliances	☐	☐	☐
Island	☐	☐	☐

	Good	Average	Poor
Basement	☐	☐	☐
Garage	☐	☐	☐

COMMUNITY

	Good	Average	Poor
Immediate Neighborhood	☐	☐	☐
Close to Employment	☐	☐	☐
Close to Shopping	☐	☐	☐
Close to Transportation	☐	☐	☐
Close to Schools / Daycare	☐	☐	☐
Close to Places of Worship	☐	☐	☐
Near Recreational Facilities	☐	☐	☐
Close to Airport	☐	☐	☐
Near Police and Fire Department	☐	☐	☐

Address _____   Price _____

Bedrooms _____   Bathrooms _____   Sq.Ft. _____

Lot Size: _____   Year Built _____   School District _____

Annual Tax _____

EXTERIOR

	Good	Average	Poor
View/Yard/Landscaping	☐	☐	☐
Trees	☐	☐	☐
Lawn (Front)	☐	☐	☐
Lawn (Back)	☐	☐	☐
Fences (condition)	☐	☐	☐
Landscaping (condition)	☐	☐	☐
Irrigation / Sprinkler	☐	☐	☐
	☐	☐	☐
House Type	☐	☐	☐
Exterior Siding	☐	☐	☐
Deck / Patio / Porch	☐	☐	☐
Garage	☐	☐	☐
Window / Doors	☐	☐	☐
Roof / Gutters	☐	☐	☐
Fencing	☐	☐	☐

HOME SYSTEMS

	Good	Average	Poor
Electrical	☐	☐	☐
Air Conditioning / Fans	☐	☐	☐
Heating	☐	☐	☐
Security	☐	☐	☐
Plumbing	☐	☐	☐
Intercom	☐	☐	☐

FEATURES

	Good	Average	Poor
Home Warranty	☐	☐	☐
Energy Saving Features	☐	☐	☐

INTERIOR

	Good	Average	Poor
Walls / Trim / Ceilings	☐	☐	☐
Flooring	☐	☐	☐
Stairs	☐	☐	☐
Storage	☐	☐	☐
Living Room	☐	☐	☐
Family Room	☐	☐	☐
Dining Room	☐	☐	☐

	Good	Average	Poor
Master Bedroom	☐	☐	☐
Bedroom 2	☐	☐	☐
Bedroom 3	☐	☐	☐
Bedroom 4	☐	☐	☐
Master Bathroom	☐	☐	☐
Bathroom 2	☐	☐	☐
Bathroom 3	☐	☐	☐
Bonus / Game Room	☐	☐	☐

	Good	Average	Poor
Kitchen	☐	☐	☐
Cabinets	☐	☐	☐
Countertop	☐	☐	☐
Counter Space	☐	☐	☐
Flooring	☐	☐	☐
Oven / Stove	☐	☐	☐
Microwave	☐	☐	☐
Layout	☐	☐	☐
Light Fixtures	☐	☐	☐
Backsplash	☐	☐	☐
Pantry	☐	☐	☐
Appliances	☐	☐	☐
Island	☐	☐	☐

	Good	Average	Poor
Basement	☐	☐	☐
Garage	☐	☐	☐

COMMUNITY

	Good	Average	Poor
Immediate Neighborhood	☐	☐	☐
Close to Employment	☐	☐	☐
Close to Shopping	☐	☐	☐
Close to Transportation	☐	☐	☐
Close to Schools / Daycare	☐	☐	☐
Close to Places of Worship	☐	☐	☐
Near Recreational Facilities	☐	☐	☐
Close to Airport	☐	☐	☐
Near Police and Fire Department	☐	☐	☐

Address _____ Price _____

Bedrooms _____ Bathrooms _____ Sq.Ft. _____

Lot Size: _____ Year Built _____ School District _____

Annual Tax _____

EXTERIOR

	Good	Average	Poor
View/Yard/Landscaping	☐	☐	☐
Trees	☐	☐	☐
Lawn (Front)	☐	☐	☐
Lawn (Back)	☐	☐	☐
Fences (condition)	☐	☐	☐
Landscaping (condition)	☐	☐	☐
Irrigation / Sprinkler	☐	☐	☐
	☐	☐	☐
House Type	☐	☐	☐
Exterior Siding	☐	☐	☐
Deck / Patio / Porch	☐	☐	☐
Garage	☐	☐	☐
Window / Doors	☐	☐	☐
Roof / Gutters	☐	☐	☐
Fencing	☐	☐	☐

HOME SYSTEMS

	Good	Average	Poor
Electrical	☐	☐	☐
Air Conditioning / Fans	☐	☐	☐
Heating	☐	☐	☐
Security	☐	☐	☐
Plumbing	☐	☐	☐
Intercom	☐	☐	☐

FEATURES

	Good	Average	Poor
Home Warranty	☐	☐	☐
Energy Saving Features	☐	☐	☐

INTERIOR

	Good	Average	Poor
Walls / Trim / Ceilings	☐	☐	☐
Flooring	☐	☐	☐
Stairs	☐	☐	☐
Storage	☐	☐	☐
Living Room	☐	☐	☐
Family Room	☐	☐	☐
Dining Room	☐	☐	☐

	Good	Average	Poor
Master Bedroom	☐	☐	☐
Bedroom 2	☐	☐	☐
Bedroom 3	☐	☐	☐
Bedroom 4	☐	☐	☐
Master Bathroom	☐	☐	☐
Bathroom 2	☐	☐	☐
Bathroom 3	☐	☐	☐
Bonus / Game Room	☐	☐	☐

	Good	Average	Poor
Kitchen	☐	☐	☐
Cabinets	☐	☐	☐
Countertop	☐	☐	☐
Counter Space	☐	☐	☐
Flooring	☐	☐	☐
Oven / Stove	☐	☐	☐
Microwave	☐	☐	☐
Layout	☐	☐	☐
Light Fixtures	☐	☐	☐
Backsplash	☐	☐	☐
Pantry	☐	☐	☐
Appliances	☐	☐	☐
Island	☐	☐	☐

	Good	Average	Poor
Basement	☐	☐	☐
Garage	☐	☐	☐

COMMUNITY

	Good	Average	Poor
Immediate Neighborhood	☐	☐	☐
Close to Employment	☐	☐	☐
Close to Shopping	☐	☐	☐
Close to Transportation	☐	☐	☐
Close to Schools / Daycare	☐	☐	☐
Close to Places of Worship	☐	☐	☐
Near Recreational Facilities	☐	☐	☐
Close to Airport	☐	☐	☐
Near Police and Fire Department	☐	☐	☐

Address _____ Price _____

Bedrooms _____ Bathrooms _____ Sq.Ft. _____

Lot Size: _____ Year Built _____ School District _____

Annual Tax _____

EXTERIOR

	Good	Average	Poor
View/Yard/Landscaping	☐	☐	☐
Trees	☐	☐	☐
Lawn (Front)	☐	☐	☐
Lawn (Back)	☐	☐	☐
Fences (condition)	☐	☐	☐
Landscaping (condition)	☐	☐	☐
Irrigation / Sprinkler	☐	☐	☐
	☐	☐	☐
House Type	☐	☐	☐
Exterior Siding	☐	☐	☐
Deck / Patio / Porch	☐	☐	☐
Garage	☐	☐	☐
Window / Doors	☐	☐	☐
Roof / Gutters	☐	☐	☐
Fencing	☐	☐	☐

HOME SYSTEMS

	Good	Average	Poor
Electrical	☐	☐	☐
Air Conditioning / Fans	☐	☐	☐
Heating	☐	☐	☐
Security	☐	☐	☐
Plumbing	☐	☐	☐
Intercom	☐	☐	☐

FEATURES

	Good	Average	Poor
Home Warranty	☐	☐	☐
Energy Saving Features	☐	☐	☐

INTERIOR

	Good	Average	Poor
Walls / Trim / Ceilings	☐	☐	☐
Flooring	☐	☐	☐
Stairs	☐	☐	☐
Storage	☐	☐	☐
Living Room	☐	☐	☐
Family Room	☐	☐	☐
Dining Room	☐	☐	☐

	Good	Average	Poor
Master Bedroom	☐	☐	☐
Bedroom 2	☐	☐	☐
Bedroom 3	☐	☐	☐
Bedroom 4	☐	☐	☐
Master Bathroom	☐	☐	☐
Bathroom 2	☐	☐	☐
Bathroom 3	☐	☐	☐
Bonus / Game Room	☐	☐	☐

	Good	Average	Poor
Kitchen	☐	☐	☐
Cabinets	☐	☐	☐
Countertop	☐	☐	☐
Counter Space	☐	☐	☐
Flooring	☐	☐	☐
Oven / Stove	☐	☐	☐
Microwave	☐	☐	☐
Layout	☐	☐	☐
Light Fixtures	☐	☐	☐
Backsplash	☐	☐	☐
Pantry	☐	☐	☐
Appliances	☐	☐	☐
Island	☐	☐	☐

	Good	Average	Poor
Basement	☐	☐	☐
Garage	☐	☐	☐

COMMUNITY

	Good	Average	Poor
Immediate Neighborhood	☐	☐	☐
Close to Employment	☐	☐	☐
Close to Shopping	☐	☐	☐
Close to Transportation	☐	☐	☐
Close to Schools / Daycare	☐	☐	☐
Close to Places of Worship	☐	☐	☐
Near Recreational Facilities	☐	☐	☐
Close to Airport	☐	☐	☐
Near Police and Fire Department	☐	☐	☐

Address _____ Price _____

Bedrooms _____ Bathrooms _____ Sq.Ft. _____

Lot Size: _____ Year Built _____ School District _____

Annual Tax _____

EXTERIOR

	Good	Average	Poor
View/Yard/Landscaping	☐	☐	☐
Trees	☐	☐	☐
Lawn (Front)	☐	☐	☐
Lawn (Back)	☐	☐	☐
Fences (condition)	☐	☐	☐
Landscaping (condition)	☐	☐	☐
Irrigation / Sprinkler	☐	☐	☐
	☐	☐	☐
House Type	☐	☐	☐
Exterior Siding	☐	☐	☐
Deck / Patio / Porch	☐	☐	☐
Garage	☐	☐	☐
Window / Doors	☐	☐	☐
Roof / Gutters	☐	☐	☐
Fencing	☐	☐	☐

HOME SYSTEMS

	Good	Average	Poor
Electrical	☐	☐	☐
Air Conditioning / Fans	☐	☐	☐
Heating	☐	☐	☐
Security	☐	☐	☐
Plumbing	☐	☐	☐
Intercom	☐	☐	☐

FEATURES

	Good	Average	Poor
Home Warranty	☐	☐	☐
Energy Saving Features	☐	☐	☐

INTERIOR

	Good	Average	Poor
Walls / Trim / Ceilings	☐	☐	☐
Flooring	☐	☐	☐
Stairs	☐	☐	☐
Storage	☐	☐	☐
Living Room	☐	☐	☐
Family Room	☐	☐	☐
Dining Room	☐	☐	☐

	Good	Average	Poor
Master Bedroom	☐	☐	☐
Bedroom 2	☐	☐	☐
Bedroom 3	☐	☐	☐
Bedroom 4	☐	☐	☐
Master Bathroom	☐	☐	☐
Bathroom 2	☐	☐	☐
Bathroom 3	☐	☐	☐
Bonus / Game Room	☐	☐	☐

	Good	Average	Poor
Kitchen	☐	☐	☐
Cabinets	☐	☐	☐
Countertop	☐	☐	☐
Counter Space	☐	☐	☐
Flooring	☐	☐	☐
Oven / Stove	☐	☐	☐
Microwave	☐	☐	☐
Layout	☐	☐	☐
Light Fixtures	☐	☐	☐
Backsplash	☐	☐	☐
Pantry	☐	☐	☐
Appliances	☐	☐	☐
Island	☐	☐	☐

	Good	Average	Poor
Basement	☐	☐	☐
Garage	☐	☐	☐

COMMUNITY

	Good	Average	Poor
Immediate Neighborhood	☐	☐	☐
Close to Employment	☐	☐	☐
Close to Shopping	☐	☐	☐
Close to Transportation	☐	☐	☐
Close to Schools / Daycare	☐	☐	☐
Close to Places of Worship	☐	☐	☐
Near Recreational Facilities	☐	☐	☐
Close to Airport	☐	☐	☐
Near Police and Fire Department	☐	☐	☐

Address _____   Price _____

Bedrooms _____   Bathrooms _____   Sq.Ft. _____

Lot Size: _____   Year Built _____   School District _____

Annual Tax _____

EXTERIOR

	Good	Average	Poor
View/Yard/Landscaping	☐	☐	☐
Trees	☐	☐	☐
Lawn (Front)	☐	☐	☐
Lawn (Back)	☐	☐	☐
Fences (condition)	☐	☐	☐
Landscaping (condition)	☐	☐	☐
Irrigation / Sprinkler	☐	☐	☐
	☐	☐	☐
House Type	☐	☐	☐
Exterior Siding	☐	☐	☐
Deck / Patio / Porch	☐	☐	☐
Garage	☐	☐	☐
Window / Doors	☐	☐	☐
Roof / Gutters	☐	☐	☐
Fencing	☐	☐	☐

HOME SYSTEMS

	Good	Average	Poor
Electrical	☐	☐	☐
Air Conditioning / Fans	☐	☐	☐
Heating	☐	☐	☐
Security	☐	☐	☐
Plumbing	☐	☐	☐
Intercom	☐	☐	☐

FEATURES

	Good	Average	Poor
Home Warranty	☐	☐	☐
Energy Saving Features	☐	☐	☐

INTERIOR

	Good	Average	Poor
Walls / Trim / Ceilings	☐	☐	☐
Flooring	☐	☐	☐
Stairs	☐	☐	☐
Storage	☐	☐	☐
Living Room	☐	☐	☐
Family Room	☐	☐	☐
Dining Room	☐	☐	☐

	Good	Average	Poor
Master Bedroom	☐	☐	☐
Bedroom 2	☐	☐	☐
Bedroom 3	☐	☐	☐
Bedroom 4	☐	☐	☐
Master Bathroom	☐	☐	☐
Bathroom 2	☐	☐	☐
Bathroom 3	☐	☐	☐
Bonus / Game Room	☐	☐	☐

	Good	Average	Poor
Kitchen	☐	☐	☐
Cabinets	☐	☐	☐
Countertop	☐	☐	☐
Counter Space	☐	☐	☐
Flooring	☐	☐	☐
Oven / Stove	☐	☐	☐
Microwave	☐	☐	☐
Layout	☐	☐	☐
Light Fixtures	☐	☐	☐
Backsplash	☐	☐	☐
Pantry	☐	☐	☐
Appliances	☐	☐	☐
Island	☐	☐	☐

	Good	Average	Poor
Basement	☐	☐	☐
Garage	☐	☐	☐

COMMUNITY

	Good	Average	Poor
Immediate Neighborhood	☐	☐	☐
Close to Employment	☐	☐	☐
Close to Shopping	☐	☐	☐
Close to Transportation	☐	☐	☐
Close to Schools / Daycare	☐	☐	☐
Close to Places of Worship	☐	☐	☐
Near Recreational Facilities	☐	☐	☐
Close to Airport	☐	☐	☐
Near Police and Fire Department	☐	☐	

Address _____ Price _____

Bedrooms _____ Bathrooms _____ Sq.Ft. _____

Lot Size: _____ Year Built _____ School District _____

Annual Tax _____

EXTERIOR

	Good	Average	Poor
View/Yard/Landscaping	☐	☐	☐
Trees	☐	☐	☐
Lawn (Front)	☐	☐	☐
Lawn (Back)	☐	☐	☐
Fences (condition)	☐	☐	☐
Landscaping (condition)	☐	☐	☐
Irrigation / Sprinkler	☐	☐	☐
	☐	☐	☐
House Type	☐	☐	☐
Exterior Siding	☐	☐	☐
Deck / Patio / Porch	☐	☐	☐
Garage	☐	☐	☐
Window / Doors	☐	☐	☐
Roof / Gutters	☐	☐	☐
Fencing	☐	☐	☐

	Good	Average	Poor
Master Bedroom	☐	☐	☐
Bedroom 2	☐	☐	☐
Bedroom 3	☐	☐	☐
Bedroom 4	☐	☐	☐
Master Bathroom	☐	☐	☐
Bathroom 2	☐	☐	☐
Bathroom 3	☐	☐	☐
Bonus / Game Room	☐	☐	☐

	Good	Average	Poor
Kitchen	☐	☐	☐
Cabinets	☐	☐	☐
Countertop	☐	☐	☐
Counter Space	☐	☐	☐
Flooring	☐	☐	☐
Oven / Stove	☐	☐	☐
Microwave	☐	☐	☐
Layout	☐	☐	☐
Light Fixtures	☐	☐	☐
Backsplash	☐	☐	☐
Pantry	☐	☐	☐
Appliances	☐	☐	☐
Island	☐	☐	☐

	Good	Average	Poor
Basement	☐	☐	☐
Garage	☐	☐	☐

HOME SYSTEMS

	Good	Average	Poor
Electrical	☐	☐	☐
Air Conditioning / Fans	☐	☐	☐
Heating	☐	☐	☐
Security	☐	☐	☐
Plumbing	☐	☐	☐
Intercom	☐	☐	☐

FEATURES

	Good	Average	Poor
Home Warranty	☐	☐	☐
Energy Saving Features	☐	☐	☐

INTERIOR

	Good	Average	Poor
Walls / Trim / Ceilings	☐	☐	☐
Flooring	☐	☐	☐
Stairs	☐	☐	☐
Storage	☐	☐	☐
Living Room	☐	☐	☐
Family Room	☐	☐	☐
Dining Room	☐	☐	☐

COMMUNITY

	Good	Average	Poor
Immediate Neighborhood	☐	☐	☐
Close to Employment	☐	☐	☐
Close to Shopping	☐	☐	☐
Close to Transportation	☐	☐	☐
Close to Schools / Daycare	☐	☐	☐
Close to Places of Worship	☐	☐	☐
Near Recreational Facilities	☐	☐	☐
Close to Airport	☐	☐	☐
Near Police and Fire Department	☐	☐	☐

Address _____ Price _____

Bedrooms _____ Bathrooms _____ Sq.Ft. _____

Lot Size: _____ Year Built _____ School District _____

Annual Tax _____

EXTERIOR

	Good	Average	Poor
View/Yard/Landscaping	☐	☐	☐
Trees	☐	☐	☐
Lawn (Front)	☐	☐	☐
Lawn (Back)	☐	☐	☐
Fences (condition)	☐	☐	☐
Landscaping (condition)	☐	☐	☐
Irrigation / Sprinkler	☐	☐	☐
	☐	☐	☐
House Type	☐	☐	☐
Exterior Siding	☐	☐	☐
Deck / Patio / Porch	☐	☐	☐
Garage	☐	☐	☐
Window / Doors	☐	☐	☐
Roof / Gutters	☐	☐	☐
Fencing	☐	☐	☐

HOME SYSTEMS

	Good	Average	Poor
Electrical	☐	☐	☐
Air Conditioning / Fans	☐	☐	☐
Heating	☐	☐	☐
Security	☐	☐	☐
Plumbing	☐	☐	☐
Intercom	☐	☐	☐

FEATURES

	Good	Average	Poor
Home Warranty	☐	☐	☐
Energy Saving Features	☐	☐	☐

INTERIOR

	Good	Average	Poor
Walls / Trim / Ceilings	☐	☐	☐
Flooring	☐	☐	☐
Stairs	☐	☐	☐
Storage	☐	☐	☐
Living Room	☐	☐	☐
Family Room	☐	☐	☐
Dining Room	☐	☐	☐

	Good	Average	Poor
Master Bedroom	☐	☐	☐
Bedroom 2	☐	☐	☐
Bedroom 3	☐	☐	☐
Bedroom 4	☐	☐	☐
Master Bathroom	☐	☐	☐
Bathroom 2	☐	☐	☐
Bathroom 3	☐	☐	☐
Bonus / Game Room	☐	☐	☐

	Good	Average	Poor
Kitchen	☐	☐	☐
Cabinets	☐	☐	☐
Countertop	☐	☐	☐
Counter Space	☐	☐	☐
Flooring	☐	☐	☐
Oven / Stove	☐	☐	☐
Microwave	☐	☐	☐
Layout	☐	☐	☐
Light Fixtures	☐	☐	☐
Backsplash	☐	☐	☐
Pantry	☐	☐	☐
Appliances	☐	☐	☐
Island	☐	☐	☐

	Good	Average	Poor
Basement	☐	☐	☐
Garage	☐	☐	☐

COMMUNITY

	Good	Average	Poor
Immediate Neighborhood	☐	☐	☐
Close to Employment	☐	☐	☐
Close to Shopping	☐	☐	☐
Close to Transportation	☐	☐	☐
Close to Schools / Daycare	☐	☐	☐
Close to Places of Worship	☐	☐	☐
Near Recreational Facilities	☐	☐	☐
Close to Airport	☐	☐	☐
Near Police and Fire Department	☐	☐	☐

71

Address _____ Price _____

Bedrooms _____ Bathrooms _____ Sq.Ft. _____

Lot Size: _____ Year Built _____ School District _____

Annual Tax _____

EXTERIOR

	Good	Average	Poor
View/Yard/Landscaping	☐	☐	☐
Trees	☐	☐	☐
Lawn (Front)	☐	☐	☐
Lawn (Back)	☐	☐	☐
Fences (condition)	☐	☐	☐
Landscaping (condition)	☐	☐	☐
Irrigation / Sprinkler	☐	☐	☐
	☐	☐	☐
House Type	☐	☐	☐
Exterior Siding	☐	☐	☐
Deck / Patio / Porch	☐	☐	☐
Garage	☐	☐	☐
Window / Doors	☐	☐	☐
Roof / Gutters	☐	☐	☐
Fencing	☐	☐	☐

HOME SYSTEMS

	Good	Average	Poor
Electrical	☐	☐	☐
Air Conditioning / Fans	☐	☐	☐
Heating	☐	☐	☐
Security	☐	☐	☐
Plumbing	☐	☐	☐
Intercom	☐	☐	☐

FEATURES

	Good	Average	Poor
Home Warranty	☐	☐	☐
Energy Saving Features	☐	☐	☐

INTERIOR

	Good	Average	Poor
Walls / Trim / Ceilings	☐	☐	☐
Flooring	☐	☐	☐
Stairs	☐	☐	☐
Storage	☐	☐	☐
Living Room	☐	☐	☐
Family Room	☐	☐	☐
Dining Room	☐	☐	☐

	Good	Average	Poor
Master Bedroom	☐	☐	☐
Bedroom 2	☐	☐	☐
Bedroom 3	☐	☐	☐
Bedroom 4	☐	☐	☐
Master Bathroom	☐	☐	☐
Bathroom 2	☐	☐	☐
Bathroom 3	☐	☐	☐
Bonus / Game Room	☐	☐	☐

	Good	Average	Poor
Kitchen	☐	☐	☐
Cabinets	☐	☐	☐
Countertop	☐	☐	☐
Counter Space	☐	☐	☐
Flooring	☐	☐	☐
Oven / Stove	☐	☐	☐
Microwave	☐	☐	☐
Layout	☐	☐	☐
Light Fixtures	☐	☐	☐
Backsplash	☐	☐	☐
Pantry	☐	☐	☐
Appliances	☐	☐	☐
Island	☐	☐	☐

	Good	Average	Poor
Basement	☐	☐	☐
Garage	☐	☐	☐

COMMUNITY

	Good	Average	Poor
Immediate Neighborhood	☐	☐	☐
Close to Employment	☐	☐	☐
Close to Shopping	☐	☐	☐
Close to Transportation	☐	☐	☐
Close to Schools / Daycare	☐	☐	☐
Close to Places of Worship	☐	☐	☐
Near Recreational Facilities	☐	☐	☐
Close to Airport	☐	☐	☐
Near Police and Fire Department	☐	☐	☐

Address _____ Price _____

Bedrooms _____ Bathrooms _____ Sq.Ft. _____

Lot Size: _____ Year Built _____ School District _____

Annual Tax _____

EXTERIOR

	Good	Average	Poor
View/Yard/Landscaping	☐	☐	☐
Trees	☐	☐	☐
Lawn (Front)	☐	☐	☐
Lawn (Back)	☐	☐	☐
Fences (condition)	☐	☐	☐
Landscaping (condition)	☐	☐	☐
Irrigation / Sprinkler	☐	☐	☐
	☐	☐	☐
House Type	☐	☐	☐
Exterior Siding	☐	☐	☐
Deck / Patio / Porch	☐	☐	☐
Garage	☐	☐	☐
Window / Doors	☐	☐	☐
Roof / Gutters	☐	☐	☐
Fencing	☐	☐	☐

HOME SYSTEMS

	Good	Average	Poor
Electrical	☐	☐	☐
Air Conditioning / Fans	☐	☐	☐
Heating	☐	☐	☐
Security	☐	☐	☐
Plumbing	☐	☐	☐
Intercom	☐	☐	☐

FEATURES

	Good	Average	Poor
Home Warranty	☐	☐	☐
Energy Saving Features	☐	☐	☐

INTERIOR

	Good	Average	Poor
Walls / Trim / Ceilings	☐	☐	☐
Flooring	☐	☐	☐
Stairs	☐	☐	☐
Storage	☐	☐	☐
Living Room	☐	☐	☐
Family Room	☐	☐	☐
Dining Room	☐	☐	☐

	Good	Average	Poor
Master Bedroom	☐	☐	☐
Bedroom 2	☐	☐	☐
Bedroom 3	☐	☐	☐
Bedroom 4	☐	☐	☐
Master Bathroom	☐	☐	☐
Bathroom 2	☐	☐	☐
Bathroom 3	☐	☐	☐
Bonus / Game Room	☐	☐	☐

	Good	Average	Poor
Kitchen	☐	☐	☐
Cabinets	☐	☐	☐
Countertop	☐	☐	☐
Counter Space	☐	☐	☐
Flooring	☐	☐	☐
Oven / Stove	☐	☐	☐
Microwave	☐	☐	☐
Layout	☐	☐	☐
Light Fixtures	☐	☐	☐
Backsplash	☐	☐	☐
Pantry	☐	☐	☐
Appliances	☐	☐	☐
Island	☐	☐	☐

	Good	Average	Poor
Basement	☐	☐	☐
Garage	☐	☐	☐

COMMUNITY

	Good	Average	Poor
Immediate Neighborhood	☐	☐	☐
Close to Employment	☐	☐	☐
Close to Shopping	☐	☐	☐
Close to Transportation	☐	☐	☐
Close to Schools / Daycare	☐	☐	☐
Close to Places of Worship	☐	☐	☐
Near Recreational Facilities	☐	☐	☐
Close to Airport	☐	☐	☐
Near Police and Fire Department	☐	☐	☐

Address _____   Price _____

Bedrooms _____   Bathrooms _____   Sq.Ft. _____

Lot Size: _____   Year Built _____   School District _____

Annual Tax _____

EXTERIOR

	Good	Average	Poor
View/Yard/Landscaping	☐	☐	☐
Trees	☐	☐	☐
Lawn (Front)	☐	☐	☐
Lawn (Back)	☐	☐	☐
Fences (condition)	☐	☐	☐
Landscaping (condition)	☐	☐	☐
Irrigation / Sprinkler	☐	☐	☐
	☐	☐	☐
House Type	☐	☐	☐
Exterior Siding	☐	☐	☐
Deck / Patio / Porch	☐	☐	☐
Garage	☐	☐	☐
Window / Doors	☐	☐	☐
Roof / Gutters	☐	☐	☐
Fencing	☐	☐	☐

HOME SYSTEMS

	Good	Average	Poor
Electrical	☐	☐	☐
Air Conditioning / Fans	☐	☐	☐
Heating	☐	☐	☐
Security	☐	☐	☐
Plumbing	☐	☐	☐
Intercom	☐	☐	☐

FEATURES

	Good	Average	Poor
Home Warranty	☐	☐	☐
Energy Saving Features	☐	☐	☐

INTERIOR

	Good	Average	Poor
Walls / Trim / Ceilings	☐	☐	☐
Flooring	☐	☐	☐
Stairs	☐	☐	☐
Storage	☐	☐	☐
Living Room	☐	☐	☐
Family Room	☐	☐	☐
Dining Room	☐	☐	☐

	Good	Average	Poor
Master Bedroom	☐	☐	☐
Bedroom 2	☐	☐	☐
Bedroom 3	☐	☐	☐
Bedroom 4	☐	☐	☐
Master Bathroom	☐	☐	☐
Bathroom 2	☐	☐	☐
Bathroom 3	☐	☐	☐
Bonus / Game Room	☐	☐	☐

	Good	Average	Poor
Kitchen	☐	☐	☐
Cabinets	☐	☐	☐
Countertop	☐	☐	☐
Counter Space	☐	☐	☐
Flooring	☐	☐	☐
Oven / Stove	☐	☐	☐
Microwave	☐	☐	☐
Layout	☐	☐	☐
Light Fixtures	☐	☐	☐
Backsplash	☐	☐	☐
Pantry	☐	☐	☐
Appliances	☐	☐	☐
Island	☐	☐	☐

	Good	Average	Poor
Basement	☐	☐	☐
Garage	☐	☐	☐

COMMUNITY

	Good	Average	Poor
Immediate Neighborhood	☐	☐	☐
Close to Employment	☐	☐	☐
Close to Shopping	☐	☐	☐
Close to Transportation	☐	☐	☐
Close to Schools / Daycare	☐	☐	☐
Close to Places of Worship	☐	☐	☐
Near Recreational Facilities	☐	☐	☐
Close to Airport	☐	☐	☐
Near Police and Fire Department	☐	☐	☐

Address _____ Price _____

Bedrooms _____ Bathrooms _____ Sq.Ft. _____

Lot Size: _____ Year Built _____ School District _____

Annual Tax _____

EXTERIOR

	Good	Average	Poor
View/Yard/Landscaping	☐	☐	☐
Trees	☐	☐	☐
Lawn (Front)	☐	☐	☐
Lawn (Back)	☐	☐	☐
Fences (condition)	☐	☐	☐
Landscaping (condition)	☐	☐	☐
Irrigation / Sprinkler	☐	☐	☐
	☐	☐	☐
House Type	☐	☐	☐
Exterior Siding	☐	☐	☐
Deck / Patio / Porch	☐	☐	☐
Garage	☐	☐	☐
Window / Doors	☐	☐	☐
Roof / Gutters	☐	☐	☐
Fencing	☐	☐	☐

	Good	Average	Poor
Master Bedroom	☐	☐	☐
Bedroom 2	☐	☐	☐
Bedroom 3	☐	☐	☐
Bedroom 4	☐	☐	☐
Master Bathroom	☐	☐	☐
Bathroom 2	☐	☐	☐
Bathroom 3	☐	☐	☐
Bonus / Game Room	☐	☐	☐

	Good	Average	Poor
Kitchen	☐	☐	☐
Cabinets	☐	☐	☐
Countertop	☐	☐	☐
Counter Space	☐	☐	☐
Flooring	☐	☐	☐
Oven / Stove	☐	☐	☐
Microwave	☐	☐	☐
Layout	☐	☐	☐
Light Fixtures	☐	☐	☐
Backsplash	☐	☐	☐
Pantry	☐	☐	☐
Appliances	☐	☐	☐
Island	☐	☐	☐

HOME SYSTEMS

	Good	Average	Poor
Electrical	☐	☐	☐
Air Conditioning / Fans	☐	☐	☐
Heating	☐	☐	☐
Security	☐	☐	☐
Plumbing	☐	☐	☐
Intercom	☐	☐	☐

	Good	Average	Poor
Basement	☐	☐	☐
Garage	☐	☐	☐

FEATURES

	Good	Average	Poor
Home Warranty	☐	☐	☐
Energy Saving Features	☐	☐	☐

INTERIOR

	Good	Average	Poor
Walls / Trim / Ceilings	☐	☐	☐
Flooring	☐	☐	☐
Stairs	☐	☐	☐
Storage	☐	☐	☐
Living Room	☐	☐	☐
Family Room	☐	☐	☐
Dining Room	☐	☐	☐

COMMUNITY

	Good	Average	Poor
Immediate Neighborhood	☐	☐	☐
Close to Employment	☐	☐	☐
Close to Shopping	☐	☐	☐
Close to Transportation	☐	☐	☐
Close to Schools / Daycare	☐	☐	☐
Close to Places of Worship	☐	☐	☐
Near Recreational Facilities	☐	☐	☐
Close to Airport	☐	☐	☐
Near Police and Fire Department	☐	☐	☐

Address _____ Price _____

Bedrooms _____ Bathrooms _____ Sq.Ft. _____

Lot Size: _____ Year Built _____ School District _____

Annual Tax _____

EXTERIOR

	Good	Average	Poor
View/Yard/Landscaping	☐	☐	☐
Trees	☐	☐	☐
Lawn (Front)	☐	☐	☐
Lawn (Back)	☐	☐	☐
Fences (condition)	☐	☐	☐
Landscaping (condition)	☐	☐	☐
Irrigation / Sprinkler	☐	☐	☐
House Type	☐	☐	☐
Exterior Siding	☐	☐	☐
Deck / Patio / Porch	☐	☐	☐
Garage	☐	☐	☐
Window / Doors	☐	☐	☐
Roof / Gutters	☐	☐	☐
Fencing	☐	☐	☐

HOME SYSTEMS

	Good	Average	Poor
Electrical	☐	☐	☐
Air Conditioning / Fans	☐	☐	☐
Heating	☐	☐	☐
Security	☐	☐	☐
Plumbing	☐	☐	☐
Intercom	☐	☐	☐

FEATURES

	Good	Average	Poor
Home Warranty	☐	☐	☐
Energy Saving Features	☐	☐	☐

INTERIOR

	Good	Average	Poor
Walls / Trim / Ceilings	☐	☐	☐
Flooring	☐	☐	☐
Stairs	☐	☐	☐
Storage	☐	☐	☐
Living Room	☐	☐	☐
Family Room	☐	☐	☐
Dining Room	☐	☐	☐

	Good	Average	Poor
Master Bedroom	☐	☐	☐
Bedroom 2	☐	☐	☐
Bedroom 3	☐	☐	☐
Bedroom 4	☐	☐	☐
Master Bathroom	☐	☐	☐
Bathroom 2	☐	☐	☐
Bathroom 3	☐	☐	☐
Bonus / Game Room	☐	☐	☐

	Good	Average	Poor
Kitchen	☐	☐	☐
Cabinets	☐	☐	☐
Countertop	☐	☐	☐
Counter Space	☐	☐	☐
Flooring	☐	☐	☐
Oven / Stove	☐	☐	☐
Microwave	☐	☐	☐
Layout	☐	☐	☐
Light Fixtures	☐	☐	☐
Backsplash	☐	☐	☐
Pantry	☐	☐	☐
Appliances	☐	☐	☐
Island	☐	☐	☐

	Good	Average	Poor
Basement	☐	☐	☐
Garage	☐	☐	☐

COMMUNITY

	Good	Average	Poor
Immediate Neighborhood	☐	☐	☐
Close to Employment	☐	☐	☐
Close to Shopping	☐	☐	☐
Close to Transportation	☐	☐	☐
Close to Schools / Daycare	☐	☐	☐
Close to Places of Worship	☐	☐	☐
Near Recreational Facilities	☐	☐	☐
Close to Airport	☐	☐	☐
Near Police and Fire Department	☐	☐	☐

76

Address _____   Price _____

Bedrooms _____   Bathrooms _____   Sq.Ft. _____

Lot Size: _____   Year Built _____   School District _____

Annual Tax _____

EXTERIOR

	Good	Average	Poor
View/Yard/Landscaping	☐	☐	☐
Trees	☐	☐	☐
Lawn (Front)	☐	☐	☐
Lawn (Back)	☐	☐	☐
Fences (condition)	☐	☐	☐
Landscaping (condition)	☐	☐	☐
Irrigation / Sprinkler	☐	☐	☐
	☐	☐	☐
House Type	☐	☐	☐
Exterior Siding	☐	☐	☐
Deck / Patio / Porch	☐	☐	☐
Garage	☐	☐	☐
Window / Doors	☐	☐	☐
Roof / Gutters	☐	☐	☐
Fencing	☐	☐	☐

HOME SYSTEMS

	Good	Average	Poor
Electrical	☐	☐	☐
Air Conditioning / Fans	☐	☐	☐
Heating	☐	☐	☐
Security	☐	☐	☐
Plumbing	☐	☐	☐
Intercom	☐	☐	☐

FEATURES

	Good	Average	Poor
Home Warranty	☐	☐	☐
Energy Saving Features	☐	☐	☐

INTERIOR

	Good	Average	Poor
Walls / Trim / Ceilings	☐	☐	☐
Flooring	☐	☐	☐
Stairs	☐	☐	☐
Storage	☐	☐	☐
Living Room	☐	☐	☐
Family Room	☐	☐	☐
Dining Room	☐	☐	☐

	Good	Average	Poor
Master Bedroom	☐	☐	☐
Bedroom 2	☐	☐	☐
Bedroom 3	☐	☐	☐
Bedroom 4	☐	☐	☐
Master Bathroom	☐	☐	☐
Bathroom 2	☐	☐	☐
Bathroom 3	☐	☐	☐
Bonus / Game Room	☐	☐	☐

	Good	Average	Poor
Kitchen	☐	☐	☐
Cabinets	☐	☐	☐
Countertop	☐	☐	☐
Counter Space	☐	☐	☐
Flooring	☐	☐	☐
Oven / Stove	☐	☐	☐
Microwave	☐	☐	☐
Layout	☐	☐	☐
Light Fixtures	☐	☐	☐
Backsplash	☐	☐	☐
Pantry	☐	☐	☐
Appliances	☐	☐	☐
Island	☐	☐	☐

	Good	Average	Poor
Basement	☐	☐	☐
Garage	☐	☐	☐

COMMUNITY

	Good	Average	Poor
Immediate Neighborhood	☐	☐	☐
Close to Employment	☐	☐	☐
Close to Shopping	☐	☐	☐
Close to Transportation	☐	☐	☐
Close to Schools / Daycare	☐	☐	☐
Close to Places of Worship	☐	☐	☐
Near Recreational Facilities	☐	☐	☐
Close to Airport	☐	☐	☐
Near Police and Fire Department	☐	☐	☐

Address _____   Price _____

Bedrooms _____   Bathrooms _____   Sq.Ft. _____

Lot Size: _____   Year Built _____   School District _____

Annual Tax _____

EXTERIOR

	Good	Average	Poor
View/Yard/Landscaping	☐	☐	☐
Trees	☐	☐	☐
Lawn (Front)	☐	☐	☐
Lawn (Back)	☐	☐	☐
Fences (condition)	☐	☐	☐
Landscaping (condition)	☐	☐	☐
Irrigation / Sprinkler	☐	☐	☐
House Type	☐	☐	☐
Exterior Siding	☐	☐	☐
Deck / Patio / Porch	☐	☐	☐
Garage	☐	☐	☐
Window / Doors	☐	☐	☐
Roof / Gutters	☐	☐	☐
Fencing	☐	☐	☐

HOME SYSTEMS

	Good	Average	Poor
Electrical	☐	☐	☐
Air Conditioning / Fans	☐	☐	☐
Heating	☐	☐	☐
Security	☐	☐	☐
Plumbing	☐	☐	☐
Intercom	☐	☐	☐

FEATURES

	Good	Average	Poor
Home Warranty	☐	☐	☐
Energy Saving Features	☐	☐	☐

INTERIOR

	Good	Average	Poor
Walls / Trim / Ceilings	☐	☐	☐
Flooring	☐	☐	☐
Stairs	☐	☐	☐
Storage	☐	☐	☐
Living Room	☐	☐	☐
Family Room	☐	☐	☐
Dining Room	☐	☐	☐

	Good	Average	Poor
Master Bedroom	☐	☐	☐
Bedroom 2	☐	☐	☐
Bedroom 3	☐	☐	☐
Bedroom 4	☐	☐	☐
Master Bathroom	☐	☐	☐
Bathroom 2	☐	☐	☐
Bathroom 3	☐	☐	☐
Bonus / Game Room	☐	☐	☐

	Good	Average	Poor
Kitchen	☐	☐	☐
Cabinets	☐	☐	☐
Countertop	☐	☐	☐
Counter Space	☐	☐	☐
Flooring	☐	☐	☐
Oven / Stove	☐	☐	☐
Microwave	☐	☐	☐
Layout	☐	☐	☐
Light Fixtures	☐	☐	☐
Backsplash	☐	☐	☐
Pantry	☐	☐	☐
Appliances	☐	☐	☐
Island	☐	☐	☐

	Good	Average	Poor
Basement	☐	☐	☐
Garage	☐	☐	☐

COMMUNITY

	Good	Average	Poor
Immediate Neighborhood	☐	☐	☐
Close to Employment	☐	☐	☐
Close to Shopping	☐	☐	☐
Close to Transportation	☐	☐	☐
Close to Schools / Daycare	☐	☐	☐
Close to Places of Worship	☐	☐	☐
Near Recreational Facilities	☐	☐	☐
Close to Airport	☐	☐	☐
Near Police and Fire Department	☐	☐	☐

Address _____   Price _____

Bedrooms _____ Bathrooms _____ Sq.Ft. _____

Lot Size: _____ Year Built _____ School District _____

Annual Tax _____

EXTERIOR

	Good	Average	Poor
View/Yard/Landscaping	☐	☐	☐
Trees	☐	☐	☐
Lawn (Front)	☐	☐	☐
Lawn (Back)	☐	☐	☐
Fences (condition)	☐	☐	☐
Landscaping (condition)	☐	☐	☐
Irrigation / Sprinkler	☐	☐	☐
House Type	☐	☐	☐
Exterior Siding	☐	☐	☐
Deck / Patio / Porch	☐	☐	☐
Garage	☐	☐	☐
Window / Doors	☐	☐	☐
Roof / Gutters	☐	☐	☐
Fencing	☐	☐	☐

	Good	Average	Poor
Master Bedroom	☐	☐	☐
Bedroom 2	☐	☐	☐
Bedroom 3	☐	☐	☐
Bedroom 4	☐	☐	☐
Master Bathroom	☐	☐	☐
Bathroom 2	☐	☐	☐
Bathroom 3	☐	☐	☐
Bonus / Game Room	☐	☐	☐

Kitchen	Good	Average	Poor
Cabinets	☐	☐	☐
Countertop	☐	☐	☐
Counter Space	☐	☐	☐
Flooring	☐	☐	☐
Oven / Stove	☐	☐	☐
Microwave	☐	☐	☐
Layout	☐	☐	☐
Light Fixtures	☐	☐	☐
Backsplash	☐	☐	☐
Pantry	☐	☐	☐
Appliances	☐	☐	☐
Island	☐	☐	☐

HOME SYSTEMS

	Good	Average	Poor
Electrical	☐	☐	☐
Air Conditioning / Fans	☐	☐	☐
Heating	☐	☐	☐
Security	☐	☐	☐
Plumbing	☐	☐	☐
Intercom	☐	☐	☐

	Good	Average	Poor
Basement	☐	☐	☐
Garage	☐	☐	☐

FEATURES

	Good	Average	Poor
Home Warranty	☐	☐	☐
Energy Saving Features	☐	☐	☐

COMMUNITY

	Good	Average	Poor
Immediate Neighborhood	☐	☐	☐
Close to Employment	☐	☐	☐
Close to Shopping	☐	☐	☐
Close to Transportation	☐	☐	☐
Close to Schools / Daycare	☐	☐	☐
Close to Places of Worship	☐	☐	☐
Near Recreational Facilities	☐	☐	☐
Close to Airport	☐	☐	☐
Near Police and Fire Department	☐	☐	☐

INTERIOR

	Good	Average	Poor
Walls / Trim / Ceilings	☐	☐	☐
Flooring	☐	☐	☐
Stairs	☐	☐	☐
Storage	☐	☐	☐
Living Room	☐	☐	☐
Family Room	☐	☐	☐
Dining Room	☐	☐	☐

Address _____ Price _____

Bedrooms _____ Bathrooms _____ Sq.Ft. _____

Lot Size: _____ Year Built _____ School District _____

Annual Tax _____

EXTERIOR

	Good	Average	Poor
View/Yard/Landscaping	☐	☐	☐
Trees	☐	☐	☐
Lawn (Front)	☐	☐	☐
Lawn (Back)	☐	☐	☐
Fences (condition)	☐	☐	☐
Landscaping (condition)	☐	☐	☐
Irrigation / Sprinkler	☐	☐	☐
House Type	☐	☐	☐
Exterior Siding	☐	☐	☐
Deck / Patio / Porch	☐	☐	☐
Garage	☐	☐	☐
Window / Doors	☐	☐	☐
Roof / Gutters	☐	☐	☐
Fencing	☐	☐	☐

HOME SYSTEMS

	Good	Average	Poor
Electrical	☐	☐	☐
Air Conditioning / Fans	☐	☐	☐
Heating	☐	☐	☐
Security	☐	☐	☐
Plumbing	☐	☐	☐
Intercom	☐	☐	☐

FEATURES

	Good	Average	Poor
Home Warranty	☐	☐	☐
Energy Saving Features	☐	☐	☐

INTERIOR

	Good	Average	Poor
Walls / Trim / Ceilings	☐	☐	☐
Flooring	☐	☐	☐
Stairs	☐	☐	☐
Storage	☐	☐	☐
Living Room	☐	☐	☐
Family Room	☐	☐	☐
Dining Room	☐	☐	☐

	Good	Average	Poor
Master Bedroom	☐	☐	☐
Bedroom 2	☐	☐	☐
Bedroom 3	☐	☐	☐
Bedroom 4	☐	☐	☐
Master Bathroom	☐	☐	☐
Bathroom 2	☐	☐	☐
Bathroom 3	☐	☐	☐
Bonus / Game Room	☐	☐	☐

	Good	Average	Poor
Kitchen	☐	☐	☐
Cabinets	☐	☐	☐
Countertop	☐	☐	☐
Counter Space	☐	☐	☐
Flooring	☐	☐	☐
Oven / Stove	☐	☐	☐
Microwave	☐	☐	☐
Layout	☐	☐	☐
Light Fixtures	☐	☐	☐
Backsplash	☐	☐	☐
Pantry	☐	☐	☐
Appliances	☐	☐	☐
Island	☐	☐	☐

	Good	Average	Poor
Basement	☐	☐	☐
Garage	☐	☐	☐

COMMUNITY

	Good	Average	Poor
Immediate Neighborhood	☐	☐	☐
Close to Employment	☐	☐	☐
Close to Shopping	☐	☐	☐
Close to Transportation	☐	☐	☐
Close to Schools / Daycare	☐	☐	☐
Close to Places of Worship	☐	☐	☐
Near Recreational Facilities	☐	☐	☐
Close to Airport	☐	☐	☐
Near Police and Fire Department	☐	☐	☐

Address _____   Price _____

Bedrooms _____ Bathrooms _____ Sq.Ft. _____

Lot Size: _____ Year Built _____ School District _____

Annual Tax _____

EXTERIOR

	Good	Average	Poor
View/Yard/Landscaping	☐	☐	☐
Trees	☐	☐	☐
Lawn (Front)	☐	☐	☐
Lawn (Back)	☐	☐	☐
Fences (condition)	☐	☐	☐
Landscaping (condition)	☐	☐	☐
Irrigation / Sprinkler	☐	☐	☐
	☐	☐	☐
House Type	☐	☐	☐
Exterior Siding	☐	☐	☐
Deck / Patio / Porch	☐	☐	☐
Garage	☐	☐	☐
Window / Doors	☐	☐	☐
Roof / Gutters	☐	☐	☐
Fencing	☐	☐	☐

HOME SYSTEMS

	Good	Average	Poor
Electrical	☐	☐	☐
Air Conditioning / Fans	☐	☐	☐
Heating	☐	☐	☐
Security	☐	☐	☐
Plumbing	☐	☐	☐
Intercom	☐	☐	☐

FEATURES

	Good	Average	Poor
Home Warranty	☐	☐	☐
Energy Saving Features	☐	☐	☐

INTERIOR

	Good	Average	Poor
Walls / Trim / Ceilings	☐	☐	☐
Flooring	☐	☐	☐
Stairs	☐	☐	☐
Storage	☐	☐	☐
Living Room	☐	☐	☐
Family Room	☐	☐	☐
Dining Room	☐	☐	☐

	Good	Average	Poor
Master Bedroom	☐	☐	☐
Bedroom 2	☐	☐	☐
Bedroom 3	☐	☐	☐
Bedroom 4	☐	☐	☐
Master Bathroom	☐	☐	☐
Bathroom 2	☐	☐	☐
Bathroom 3	☐	☐	☐
Bonus / Game Room	☐	☐	☐

	Good	Average	Poor
Kitchen	☐	☐	☐
Cabinets	☐	☐	☐
Countertop	☐	☐	☐
Counter Space	☐	☐	☐
Flooring	☐	☐	☐
Oven / Stove	☐	☐	☐
Microwave	☐	☐	☐
Layout	☐	☐	☐
Light Fixtures	☐	☐	☐
Backsplash	☐	☐	☐
Pantry	☐	☐	☐
Appliances	☐	☐	☐
Island	☐	☐	☐

	Good	Average	Poor
Basement	☐	☐	☐
Garage	☐	☐	☐

COMMUNITY

	Good	Average	Poor
Immediate Neighborhood	☐	☐	☐
Close to Employment	☐	☐	☐
Close to Shopping	☐	☐	☐
Close to Transportation	☐	☐	☐
Close to Schools / Daycare	☐	☐	☐
Close to Places of Worship	☐	☐	☐
Near Recreational Facilities	☐	☐	☐
Close to Airport	☐	☐	☐
Near Police and Fire Department	☐	☐	☐

Address _____   Price _____

Bedrooms _____   Bathrooms _____   Sq.Ft. _____

Lot Size: _____   Year Built _____   School District _____

Annual Tax _____

EXTERIOR

	Good	Average	Poor
View/Yard/Landscaping	☐	☐	☐
Trees	☐	☐	☐
Lawn (Front)	☐	☐	☐
Lawn (Back)	☐	☐	☐
Fences (condition)	☐	☐	☐
Landscaping (condition)	☐	☐	☐
Irrigation / Sprinkler	☐	☐	☐
House Type	☐	☐	☐
Exterior Siding	☐	☐	☐
Deck / Patio / Porch	☐	☐	☐
Garage	☐	☐	☐
Window / Doors	☐	☐	☐
Roof / Gutters	☐	☐	☐
Fencing	☐	☐	☐

HOME SYSTEMS

	Good	Average	Poor
Electrical	☐	☐	☐
Air Conditioning / Fans	☐	☐	☐
Heating	☐	☐	☐
Security	☐	☐	☐
Plumbing	☐	☐	☐
Intercom	☐	☐	☐

FEATURES

	Good	Average	Poor
Home Warranty	☐	☐	☐
Energy Saving Features	☐	☐	☐

INTERIOR

	Good	Average	Poor
Walls / Trim / Ceilings	☐	☐	☐
Flooring	☐	☐	☐
Stairs	☐	☐	☐
Storage	☐	☐	☐
Living Room	☐	☐	☐
Family Room	☐	☐	☐
Dining Room	☐	☐	☐

	Good	Average	Poor
Master Bedroom	☐	☐	☐
Bedroom 2	☐	☐	☐
Bedroom 3	☐	☐	☐
Bedroom 4	☐	☐	☐
Master Bathroom	☐	☐	☐
Bathroom 2	☐	☐	☐
Bathroom 3	☐	☐	☐
Bonus / Game Room	☐	☐	☐

	Good	Average	Poor
Kitchen	☐	☐	☐
Cabinets	☐	☐	☐
Countertop	☐	☐	☐
Counter Space	☐	☐	☐
Flooring	☐	☐	☐
Oven / Stove	☐	☐	☐
Microwave	☐	☐	☐
Layout	☐	☐	☐
Light Fixtures	☐	☐	☐
Backsplash	☐	☐	☐
Pantry	☐	☐	☐
Appliances	☐	☐	☐
Island	☐	☐	☐

	Good	Average	Poor
Basement	☐	☐	☐
Garage	☐	☐	☐

COMMUNITY

	Good	Average	Poor
Immediate Neighborhood	☐	☐	☐
Close to Employment	☐	☐	☐
Close to Shopping	☐	☐	☐
Close to Transportation	☐	☐	☐
Close to Schools / Daycare	☐	☐	☐
Close to Places of Worship	☐	☐	☐
Near Recreational Facilities	☐	☐	☐
Close to Airport	☐	☐	☐
Near Police and Fire Department	☐	☐	☐

Address _____ Price _____

Bedrooms _____ Bathrooms _____ Sq.Ft. _____

Lot Size: _____ Year Built _____ School District _____

Annual Tax _____

EXTERIOR

	Good	Average	Poor
View/Yard/Landscaping	☐	☐	☐
Trees	☐	☐	☐
Lawn (Front)	☐	☐	☐
Lawn (Back)	☐	☐	☐
Fences (condition)	☐	☐	☐
Landscaping (condition)	☐	☐	☐
Irrigation / Sprinkler	☐	☐	☐
	☐	☐	☐
House Type	☐	☐	☐
Exterior Siding	☐	☐	☐
Deck / Patio / Porch	☐	☐	☐
Garage	☐	☐	☐
Window / Doors	☐	☐	☐
Roof / Gutters	☐	☐	☐
Fencing	☐	☐	☐

HOME SYSTEMS

	Good	Average	Poor
Electrical	☐	☐	☐
Air Conditioning / Fans	☐	☐	☐
Heating	☐	☐	☐
Security	☐	☐	☐
Plumbing	☐	☐	☐
Intercom	☐	☐	☐

FEATURES

	Good	Average	Poor
Home Warranty	☐	☐	☐
Energy Saving Features	☐	☐	☐

INTERIOR

	Good	Average	Poor
Walls / Trim / Ceilings	☐	☐	☐
Flooring	☐	☐	☐
Stairs	☐	☐	☐
Storage	☐	☐	☐
Living Room	☐	☐	☐
Family Room	☐	☐	☐
Dining Room	☐	☐	☐

	Good	Average	Poor
Master Bedroom	☐	☐	☐
Bedroom 2	☐	☐	☐
Bedroom 3	☐	☐	☐
Bedroom 4	☐	☐	☐
Master Bathroom	☐	☐	☐
Bathroom 2	☐	☐	☐
Bathroom 3	☐	☐	☐
Bonus / Game Room	☐	☐	☐

Kitchen	Good	Average	Poor
Cabinets	☐	☐	☐
Countertop	☐	☐	☐
Counter Space	☐	☐	☐
Flooring	☐	☐	☐
Oven / Stove	☐	☐	☐
Microwave	☐	☐	☐
Layout	☐	☐	☐
Light Fixtures	☐	☐	☐
Backsplash	☐	☐	☐
Pantry	☐	☐	☐
Appliances	☐	☐	☐
Island	☐	☐	☐

	Good	Average	Poor
Basement	☐	☐	☐
Garage	☐	☐	☐

COMMUNITY

	Good	Average	Poor
Immediate Neighborhood	☐	☐	☐
Close to Employment	☐	☐	☐
Close to Shopping	☐	☐	☐
Close to Transportation	☐	☐	☐
Close to Schools / Daycare	☐	☐	☐
Close to Places of Worship	☐	☐	☐
Near Recreational Facilities	☐	☐	☐
Close to Airport	☐	☐	☐
Near Police and Fire Department	☐	☐	☐

Address _____   Price _____

Bedrooms _____   Bathrooms _____   Sq.Ft. _____

Lot Size: _____   Year Built _____   School District _____

Annual Tax _____

EXTERIOR

	Good	Average	Poor
View/Yard/Landscaping	☐	☐	☐
Trees	☐	☐	☐
Lawn (Front)	☐	☐	☐
Lawn (Back)	☐	☐	☐
Fences (condition)	☐	☐	☐
Landscaping (condition)	☐	☐	☐
Irrigation / Sprinkler	☐	☐	☐
	☐	☐	☐
House Type	☐	☐	☐
Exterior Siding	☐	☐	☐
Deck / Patio / Porch	☐	☐	☐
Garage	☐	☐	☐
Window / Doors	☐	☐	☐
Roof / Gutters	☐	☐	☐
Fencing	☐	☐	☐

HOME SYSTEMS

	Good	Average	Poor
Electrical	☐	☐	☐
Air Conditioning / Fans	☐	☐	☐
Heating	☐	☐	☐
Security	☐	☐	☐
Plumbing	☐	☐	☐
Intercom	☐	☐	☐

FEATURES

	Good	Average	Poor
Home Warranty	☐	☐	☐
Energy Saving Features	☐	☐	☐

INTERIOR

	Good	Average	Poor
Walls / Trim / Ceilings	☐	☐	☐
Flooring	☐	☐	☐
Stairs	☐	☐	☐
Storage	☐	☐	☐
Living Room	☐	☐	☐
Family Room	☐	☐	☐
Dining Room	☐	☐	☐

	Good	Average	Poor
Master Bedroom	☐	☐	☐
Bedroom 2	☐	☐	☐
Bedroom 3	☐	☐	☐
Bedroom 4	☐	☐	☐
Master Bathroom	☐	☐	☐
Bathroom 2	☐	☐	☐
Bathroom 3	☐	☐	☐
Bonus / Game Room	☐	☐	☐

	Good	Average	Poor
Kitchen	☐	☐	☐
Cabinets	☐	☐	☐
Countertop	☐	☐	☐
Counter Space	☐	☐	☐
Flooring	☐	☐	☐
Oven / Stove	☐	☐	☐
Microwave	☐	☐	☐
Layout	☐	☐	☐
Light Fixtures	☐	☐	☐
Backsplash	☐	☐	☐
Pantry	☐	☐	☐
Appliances	☐	☐	☐
Island	☐	☐	☐

	Good	Average	Poor
Basement	☐	☐	☐
Garage	☐	☐	☐

COMMUNITY

	Good	Average	Poor
Immediate Neighborhood	☐	☐	☐
Close to Employment	☐	☐	☐
Close to Shopping	☐	☐	☐
Close to Transportation	☐	☐	☐
Close to Schools / Daycare	☐	☐	☐
Close to Places of Worship	☐	☐	☐
Near Recreational Facilities	☐	☐	☐
Close to Airport	☐	☐	☐
Near Police and Fire Department	☐	☐	☐

Address _____   Price _____

Bedrooms _____   Bathrooms _____   Sq.Ft. _____

Lot Size: _____   Year Built _____   School District _____

Annual Tax _____

EXTERIOR

	Good	Average	Poor
View/Yard/Landscaping	☐	☐	☐
Trees	☐	☐	☐
Lawn (Front)	☐	☐	☐
Lawn (Back)	☐	☐	☐
Fences (condition)	☐	☐	☐
Landscaping (condition)	☐	☐	☐
Irrigation / Sprinkler	☐	☐	☐
	☐	☐	☐
House Type	☐	☐	☐
Exterior Siding	☐	☐	☐
Deck / Patio / Porch	☐	☐	☐
Garage	☐	☐	☐
Window / Doors	☐	☐	☐
Roof / Gutters	☐	☐	☐
Fencing	☐	☐	☐

HOME SYSTEMS

	Good	Average	Poor
Electrical	☐	☐	☐
Air Conditioning / Fans	☐	☐	☐
Heating	☐	☐	☐
Security	☐	☐	☐
Plumbing	☐	☐	☐
Intercom	☐	☐	☐

FEATURES

	Good	Average	Poor
Home Warranty	☐	☐	☐
Energy Saving Features	☐	☐	☐

INTERIOR

	Good	Average	Poor
Walls / Trim / Ceilings	☐	☐	☐
Flooring	☐	☐	☐
Stairs	☐	☐	☐
Storage	☐	☐	☐
Living Room	☐	☐	☐
Family Room	☐	☐	☐
Dining Room	☐	☐	☐

	Good	Average	Poor
Master Bedroom	☐	☐	☐
Bedroom 2	☐	☐	☐
Bedroom 3	☐	☐	☐
Bedroom 4	☐	☐	☐
Master Bathroom	☐	☐	☐
Bathroom 2	☐	☐	☐
Bathroom 3	☐	☐	☐
Bonus / Game Room	☐	☐	☐

	Good	Average	Poor
Kitchen	☐	☐	☐
Cabinets	☐	☐	☐
Countertop	☐	☐	☐
Counter Space	☐	☐	☐
Flooring	☐	☐	☐
Oven / Stove	☐	☐	☐
Microwave	☐	☐	☐
Layout	☐	☐	☐
Light Fixtures	☐	☐	☐
Backsplash	☐	☐	☐
Pantry	☐	☐	☐
Appliances	☐	☐	☐
Island	☐	☐	☐

	Good	Average	Poor
Basement	☐	☐	☐
Garage	☐	☐	☐

COMMUNITY

	Good	Average	Poor
Immediate Neighborhood	☐	☐	☐
Close to Employment	☐	☐	☐
Close to Shopping	☐	☐	☐
Close to Transportation	☐	☐	☐
Close to Schools / Daycare	☐	☐	☐
Close to Places of Worship	☐	☐	☐
Near Recreational Facilities	☐	☐	☐
Close to Airport	☐	☐	☐
Near Police and Fire Department	☐	☐	☐

Address _____ Price _____

Bedrooms _____ Bathrooms _____ Sq.Ft. _____

Lot Size: _____ Year Built _____ School District _____

Annual Tax _____

EXTERIOR

	Good	Average	Poor
View/Yard/Landscaping	☐	☐	☐
Trees	☐	☐	☐
Lawn (Front)	☐	☐	☐
Lawn (Back)	☐	☐	☐
Fences (condition)	☐	☐	☐
Landscaping (condition)	☐	☐	☐
Irrigation / Sprinkler	☐	☐	☐
	☐	☐	☐
House Type	☐	☐	☐
Exterior Siding	☐	☐	☐
Deck / Patio / Porch	☐	☐	☐
Garage	☐	☐	☐
Window / Doors	☐	☐	☐
Roof / Gutters	☐	☐	☐
Fencing	☐	☐	☐

HOME SYSTEMS

	Good	Average	Poor
Electrical	☐	☐	☐
Air Conditioning / Fans	☐	☐	☐
Heating	☐	☐	☐
Security	☐	☐	☐
Plumbing	☐	☐	☐
Intercom	☐	☐	☐

FEATURES

	Good	Average	Poor
Home Warranty	☐	☐	☐
Energy Saving Features	☐	☐	☐

INTERIOR

	Good	Average	Poor
Walls / Trim / Ceilings	☐	☐	☐
Flooring	☐	☐	☐
Stairs	☐	☐	☐
Storage	☐	☐	☐
Living Room	☐	☐	☐
Family Room	☐	☐	☐
Dining Room	☐	☐	☐

	Good	Average	Poor
Master Bedroom	☐	☐	☐
Bedroom 2	☐	☐	☐
Bedroom 3	☐	☐	☐
Bedroom 4	☐	☐	☐
Master Bathroom	☐	☐	☐
Bathroom 2	☐	☐	☐
Bathroom 3	☐	☐	☐
Bonus / Game Room	☐	☐	☐

	Good	Average	Poor
Kitchen	☐	☐	☐
Cabinets	☐	☐	☐
Countertop	☐	☐	☐
Counter Space	☐	☐	☐
Flooring	☐	☐	☐
Oven / Stove	☐	☐	☐
Microwave	☐	☐	☐
Layout	☐	☐	☐
Light Fixtures	☐	☐	☐
Backsplash	☐	☐	☐
Pantry	☐	☐	☐
Appliances	☐	☐	☐
Island	☐	☐	☐

	Good	Average	Poor
Basement	☐	☐	☐
Garage	☐	☐	☐

COMMUNITY

	Good	Average	Poor
Immediate Neighborhood	☐	☐	☐
Close to Employment	☐	☐	☐
Close to Shopping	☐	☐	☐
Close to Transportation	☐	☐	☐
Close to Schools / Daycare	☐	☐	☐
Close to Places of Worship	☐	☐	☐
Near Recreational Facilities	☐	☐	☐
Close to Airport	☐	☐	☐
Near Police and Fire Department	☐	☐	☐

Address _____   Price _____

Bedrooms _____   Bathrooms _____   Sq.Ft. _____

Lot Size: _____   Year Built _____   School District _____

Annual Tax _____

EXTERIOR

	Good	Average	Poor
View/Yard/Landscaping	☐	☐	☐
Trees	☐	☐	☐
Lawn (Front)	☐	☐	☐
Lawn (Back)	☐	☐	☐
Fences (condition)	☐	☐	☐
Landscaping (condition)	☐	☐	☐
Irrigation / Sprinkler	☐	☐	☐
	☐	☐	☐
House Type	☐	☐	☐
Exterior Siding	☐	☐	☐
Deck / Patio / Porch	☐	☐	☐
Garage	☐	☐	☐
Window / Doors	☐	☐	☐
Roof / Gutters	☐	☐	☐
Fencing	☐	☐	☐

HOME SYSTEMS

	Good	Average	Poor
Electrical	☐	☐	☐
Air Conditioning / Fans	☐	☐	☐
Heating	☐	☐	☐
Security	☐	☐	☐
Plumbing	☐	☐	☐
Intercom	☐	☐	☐

FEATURES

	Good	Average	Poor
Home Warranty	☐	☐	☐
Energy Saving Features	☐	☐	☐

INTERIOR

	Good	Average	Poor
Walls / Trim / Ceilings	☐	☐	☐
Flooring	☐	☐	☐
Stairs	☐	☐	☐
Storage	☐	☐	☐
Living Room	☐	☐	☐
Family Room	☐	☐	☐
Dining Room	☐	☐	☐

	Good	Average	Poor
Master Bedroom	☐	☐	☐
Bedroom 2	☐	☐	☐
Bedroom 3	☐	☐	☐
Bedroom 4	☐	☐	☐
Master Bathroom	☐	☐	☐
Bathroom 2	☐	☐	☐
Bathroom 3	☐	☐	☐
Bonus / Game Room	☐	☐	☐

	Good	Average	Poor
Kitchen	☐	☐	☐
Cabinets	☐	☐	☐
Countertop	☐	☐	☐
Counter Space	☐	☐	☐
Flooring	☐	☐	☐
Oven / Stove	☐	☐	☐
Microwave	☐	☐	☐
Layout	☐	☐	☐
Light Fixtures	☐	☐	☐
Backsplash	☐	☐	☐
Pantry	☐	☐	☐
Appliances	☐	☐	☐
Island	☐	☐	☐

	Good	Average	Poor
Basement	☐	☐	☐
Garage	☐	☐	☐

COMMUNITY

	Good	Average	Poor
Immediate Neighborhood	☐	☐	☐
Close to Employment	☐	☐	☐
Close to Shopping	☐	☐	☐
Close to Transportation	☐	☐	☐
Close to Schools / Daycare	☐	☐	☐
Close to Places of Worship	☐	☐	☐
Near Recreational Facilities	☐	☐	☐
Close to Airport	☐	☐	☐
Near Police and Fire Department	☐	☐	☐

87

Address _____   Price _____

Bedrooms _____   Bathrooms _____   Sq.Ft. _____

Lot Size: _____   Year Built _____   School District _____

Annual Tax _____

EXTERIOR

	Good	Average	Poor
View/Yard/Landscaping	☐	☐	☐
Trees	☐	☐	☐
Lawn (Front)	☐	☐	☐
Lawn (Back)	☐	☐	☐
Fences (condition)	☐	☐	☐
Landscaping (condition)	☐	☐	☐
Irrigation / Sprinkler	☐	☐	☐
House Type	☐	☐	☐
Exterior Siding	☐	☐	☐
Deck / Patio / Porch	☐	☐	☐
Garage	☐	☐	☐
Window / Doors	☐	☐	☐
Roof / Gutters	☐	☐	☐
Fencing	☐	☐	☐

HOME SYSTEMS

	Good	Average	Poor
Electrical	☐	☐	☐
Air Conditioning / Fans	☐	☐	☐
Heating	☐	☐	☐
Security	☐	☐	☐
Plumbing	☐	☐	☐
Intercom	☐	☐	☐

FEATURES

	Good	Average	Poor
Home Warranty	☐	☐	☐
Energy Saving Features	☐	☐	☐

INTERIOR

	Good	Average	Poor
Walls / Trim / Ceilings	☐	☐	☐
Flooring	☐	☐	☐
Stairs	☐	☐	☐
Storage	☐	☐	☐
Living Room	☐	☐	☐
Family Room	☐	☐	☐
Dining Room	☐	☐	☐

	Good	Average	Poor
Master Bedroom	☐	☐	☐
Bedroom 2	☐	☐	☐
Bedroom 3	☐	☐	☐
Bedroom 4	☐	☐	☐
Master Bathroom	☐	☐	☐
Bathroom 2	☐	☐	☐
Bathroom 3	☐	☐	☐
Bonus / Game Room	☐	☐	☐

	Good	Average	Poor
Kitchen	☐	☐	☐
Cabinets	☐	☐	☐
Countertop	☐	☐	☐
Counter Space	☐	☐	☐
Flooring	☐	☐	☐
Oven / Stove	☐	☐	☐
Microwave	☐	☐	☐
Layout	☐	☐	☐
Light Fixtures	☐	☐	☐
Backsplash	☐	☐	☐
Pantry	☐	☐	☐
Appliances	☐	☐	☐
Island	☐	☐	☐

	Good	Average	Poor
Basement	☐	☐	☐
Garage	☐	☐	☐

COMMUNITY

	Good	Average	Poor
Immediate Neighborhood	☐	☐	☐
Close to Employment	☐	☐	☐
Close to Shopping	☐	☐	☐
Close to Transportation	☐	☐	☐
Close to Schools / Daycare	☐	☐	☐
Close to Places of Worship	☐	☐	☐
Near Recreational Facilities	☐	☐	☐
Close to Airport	☐	☐	☐
Near Police and Fire Department	☐	☐	☐

Address _____   Price _____

Bedrooms _____   Bathrooms _____   Sq.Ft. _____

Lot Size: _____   Year Built _____   School District _____

Annual Tax _____

EXTERIOR

	Good	Average	Poor
View/Yard/Landscaping	☐	☐	☐
Trees	☐	☐	☐
Lawn (Front)	☐	☐	☐
Lawn (Back)	☐	☐	☐
Fences (condition)	☐	☐	☐
Landscaping (condition)	☐	☐	☐
Irrigation / Sprinkler	☐	☐	☐
	☐	☐	☐
House Type	☐	☐	☐
Exterior Siding	☐	☐	☐
Deck / Patio / Porch	☐	☐	☐
Garage	☐	☐	☐
Window / Doors	☐	☐	☐
Roof / Gutters	☐	☐	☐
Fencing	☐	☐	☐

HOME SYSTEMS

	Good	Average	Poor
Electrical	☐	☐	☐
Air Conditioning / Fans	☐	☐	☐
Heating	☐	☐	☐
Security	☐	☐	☐
Plumbing	☐	☐	☐
Intercom	☐	☐	☐

FEATURES

	Good	Average	Poor
Home Warranty	☐	☐	☐
Energy Saving Features	☐	☐	☐

INTERIOR

	Good	Average	Poor
Walls / Trim / Ceilings	☐	☐	☐
Flooring	☐	☐	☐
Stairs	☐	☐	☐
Storage	☐	☐	☐
Living Room	☐	☐	☐
Family Room	☐	☐	☐
Dining Room	☐	☐	☐

	Good	Average	Poor
Master Bedroom	☐	☐	☐
Bedroom 2	☐	☐	☐
Bedroom 3	☐	☐	☐
Bedroom 4	☐	☐	☐
Master Bathroom	☐	☐	☐
Bathroom 2	☐	☐	☐
Bathroom 3	☐	☐	☐
Bonus / Game Room	☐	☐	☐

	Good	Average	Poor
Kitchen	☐	☐	☐
Cabinets	☐	☐	☐
Countertop	☐	☐	☐
Counter Space	☐	☐	☐
Flooring	☐	☐	☐
Oven / Stove	☐	☐	☐
Microwave	☐	☐	☐
Layout	☐	☐	☐
Light Fixtures	☐	☐	☐
Backsplash	☐	☐	☐
Pantry	☐	☐	☐
Appliances	☑	☐	☐
Island	☐	☐	☐

	Good	Average	Poor
Basement	☐	☐	☐
Garage	☐	☐	☐

COMMUNITY

	Good	Average	Poor
Immediate Neighborhood	☐	☐	☐
Close to Employment	☐	☐	☐
Close to Shopping	☐	☐	☐
Close to Transportation	☐	☐	☐
Close to Schools / Daycare	☐	☐	☐
Close to Places of Worship	☐	☐	☐
Near Recreational Facilities	☐	☐	☐
Close to Airport	☐	☐	☐
Near Police and Fire Department	☐	☐	☐

Address _____   Price _____

Bedrooms _____   Bathrooms _____   Sq.Ft. _____

Lot Size: _____   Year Built _____   School District _____

Annual Tax _____

EXTERIOR

	Good	Average	Poor
View/Yard/Landscaping	☐	☐	☐
Trees	☐	☐	☐
Lawn (Front)	☐	☐	☐
Lawn (Back)	☐	☐	☐
Fences (condition)	☐	☐	☐
Landscaping (condition)	☐	☐	☐
Irrigation / Sprinkler	☐	☐	☐
	☐	☐	☐
House Type	☐	☐	☐
Exterior Siding	☐	☐	☐
Deck / Patio / Porch	☐	☐	☐
Garage	☐	☐	☐
Window / Doors	☐	☐	☐
Roof / Gutters	☐	☐	☐
Fencing	☐	☐	☐

HOME SYSTEMS

	Good	Average	Poor
Electrical	☐	☐	☐
Air Conditioning / Fans	☐	☐	☐
Heating	☐	☐	☐
Security	☐	☐	☐
Plumbing	☐	☐	☐
Intercom	☐	☐	☐

FEATURES

	Good	Average	Poor
Home Warranty	☐	☐	☐
Energy Saving Features	☐	☐	☐

INTERIOR

	Good	Average	Poor
Walls / Trim / Ceilings	☐	☐	☐
Flooring	☐	☐	☐
Stairs	☐	☐	☐
Storage	☐	☐	☐
Living Room	☐	☐	☐
Family Room	☐	☐	☐
Dining Room	☐	☐	☐

	Good	Average	Poor
Master Bedroom	☐	☐	☐
Bedroom 2	☐	☐	☐
Bedroom 3	☐	☐	☐
Bedroom 4	☐	☐	☐
Master Bathroom	☐	☐	☐
Bathroom 2	☐	☐	☐
Bathroom 3	☐	☐	☐
Bonus / Game Room	☐	☐	☐

	Good	Average	Poor
Kitchen	☐	☐	☐
Cabinets	☐	☐	☐
Countertop	☐	☐	☐
Counter Space	☐	☐	☐
Flooring	☐	☐	☐
Oven / Stove	☐	☐	☐
Microwave	☐	☐	☐
Layout	☐	☐	☐
Light Fixtures	☐	☐	☐
Backsplash	☐	☐	☐
Pantry	☐	☐	☐
Appliances	☐	☐	☐
Island	☐	☐	☐

	Good	Average	Poor
Basement	☐	☐	☐
Garage	☐	☐	☐

COMMUNITY

	Good	Average	Poor
Immediate Neighborhood	☐	☐	☐
Close to Employment	☐	☐	☐
Close to Shopping	☐	☐	☐
Close to Transportation	☐	☐	☐
Close to Schools / Daycare	☐	☐	☐
Close to Places of Worship	☐	☐	☐
Near Recreational Facilities	☐	☐	☐
Close to Airport	☐	☐	☐
Near Police and Fire Department	☐	☐	☐

Address _____   Price _____

Bedrooms _____   Bathrooms _____   Sq.Ft. _____

Lot Size: _____   Year Built _____   School District _____

Annual Tax _____

EXTERIOR

	Good	Average	Poor
View/Yard/Landscaping	☐	☐	☐
Trees	☐	☐	☐
Lawn (Front)	☐	☐	☐
Lawn (Back)	☐	☐	☐
Fences (condition)	☐	☐	☐
Landscaping (condition)	☐	☐	☐
Irrigation / Sprinkler	☐	☐	☐
	☐	☐	☐
House Type	☐	☐	☐
Exterior Siding	☐	☐	☐
Deck / Patio / Porch	☐	☐	☐
Garage	☐	☐	☐
Window / Doors	☐	☐	☐
Roof / Gutters	☐	☐	☐
Fencing	☐	☐	☐

HOME SYSTEMS

	Good	Average	Poor
Electrical	☐	☐	☐
Air Conditioning / Fans	☐	☐	☐
Heating	☐	☐	☐
Security	☐	☐	☐
Plumbing	☐	☐	☐
Intercom	☐	☐	☐

FEATURES

	Good	Average	Poor
Home Warranty	☐	☐	☐
Energy Saving Features	☐	☐	☐

INTERIOR

	Good	Average	Poor
Walls / Trim / Ceilings	☐	☐	☐
Flooring	☐	☐	☐
Stairs	☐	☐	☐
Storage	☐	☐	☐
Living Room	☐	☐	☐
Family Room	☐	☐	☐
Dining Room	☐	☐	☐

	Good	Average	Poor
Master Bedroom	☐	☐	☐
Bedroom 2	☐	☐	☐
Bedroom 3	☐	☐	☐
Bedroom 4	☐	☐	☐
Master Bathroom	☐	☐	☐
Bathroom 2	☐	☐	☐
Bathroom 3	☐	☐	☐
Bonus / Game Room	☐	☐	☐

	Good	Average	Poor
Kitchen	☐	☐	☐
Cabinets	☐	☐	☐
Countertop	☐	☐	☐
Counter Space	☐	☐	☐
Flooring	☐	☐	☐
Oven / Stove	☐	☐	☐
Microwave	☐	☐	☐
Layout	☐	☐	☐
Light Fixtures	☐	☐	☐
Backsplash	☐	☐	☐
Pantry	☐	☐	☐
Appliances	☐	☐	☐
Island	☐	☐	☐

	Good	Average	Poor
Basement	☐	☐	☐
Garage	☐	☐	☐

COMMUNITY

	Good	Average	Poor
Immediate Neighborhood	☐	☐	☐
Close to Employment	☐	☐	☐
Close to Shopping	☐	☐	☐
Close to Transportation	☐	☐	☐
Close to Schools / Daycare	☐	☐	☐
Close to Places of Worship	☐	☐	☐
Near Recreational Facilities	☐	☐	☐
Close to Airport	☐	☐	☐
Near Police and Fire Department	☐	☐	☐

Address _____   Price _____

Bedrooms _____   Bathrooms _____   Sq.Ft. _____

Lot Size: _____   Year Built _____   School District _____

Annual Tax _____

EXTERIOR

	Good	Average	Poor
View/Yard/Landscaping	☐	☐	☐
Trees	☐	☐	☐
Lawn (Front)	☐	☐	☐
Lawn (Back)	☐	☐	☐
Fences (condition)	☐	☐	☐
Landscaping (condition)	☐	☐	☐
Irrigation / Sprinkler	☐	☐	☐
House Type	☐	☐	☐
Exterior Siding	☐	☐	☐
Deck / Patio / Porch	☐	☐	☐
Garage	☐	☐	☐
Window / Doors	☐	☐	☐
Roof / Gutters	☐	☐	☐
Fencing	☐	☐	☐

HOME SYSTEMS

	Good	Average	Poor
Electrical	☐	☐	☐
Air Conditioning / Fans	☐	☐	☐
Heating	☐	☐	☐
Security	☐	☐	☐
Plumbing	☐	☐	☐
Intercom	☐	☐	☐

FEATURES

	Good	Average	Poor
Home Warranty	☐	☐	☐
Energy Saving Features	☐	☐	☐

INTERIOR

	Good	Average	Poor
Walls / Trim / Ceilings	☐	☐	☐
Flooring	☐	☐	☐
Stairs	☐	☐	☐
Storage	☐	☐	☐
Living Room	☐	☐	☐
Family Room	☐	☐	☐
Dining Room	☐	☐	☐

	Good	Average	Poor
Master Bedroom	☐	☐	☐
Bedroom 2	☐	☐	☐
Bedroom 3	☐	☐	☐
Bedroom 4	☐	☐	☐
Master Bathroom	☐	☐	☐
Bathroom 2	☐	☐	☐
Bathroom 3	☐	☐	☐
Bonus / Game Room	☐	☐	☐

	Good	Average	Poor
Kitchen	☐	☐	☐
Cabinets	☐	☐	☐
Countertop	☐	☐	☐
Counter Space	☐	☐	☐
Flooring	☐	☐	☐
Oven / Stove	☐	☐	☐
Microwave	☐	☐	☐
Layout	☐	☐	☐
Light Fixtures	☐	☐	☐
Backsplash	☐	☐	☐
Pantry	☐	☐	☐
Appliances	☐	☐	☐
Island	☐	☐	☐

	Good	Average	Poor
Basement	☐	☐	☐
Garage	☐	☐	☐

COMMUNITY

	Good	Average	Poor
Immediate Neighborhood	☐	☐	☐
Close to Employment	☐	☐	☐
Close to Shopping	☐	☐	☐
Close to Transportation	☐	☐	☐
Close to Schools / Daycare	☐	☐	☐
Close to Places of Worship	☐	☐	☐
Near Recreational Facilities	☐	☐	☐
Close to Airport	☐	☐	☐
Near Police and Fire Department	☐	☐	☐

Address _____ Price _____

Bedrooms _____ Bathrooms _____ Sq.Ft. _____

Lot Size: _____ Year Built _____ School District _____

Annual Tax _____

EXTERIOR

	Good	Average	Poor
View/Yard/Landscaping	☐	☐	☐
Trees	☐	☐	☐
Lawn (Front)	☐	☐	☐
Lawn (Back)	☐	☐	☐
Fences (condition)	☐	☐	☐
Landscaping (condition)	☐	☐	☐
Irrigation / Sprinkler	☐	☐	☐
	☐	☐	☐
House Type	☐	☐	☐
Exterior Siding	☐	☐	☐
Deck / Patio / Porch	☐	☐	☐
Garage	☐	☐	☐
Window / Doors	☐	☐	☐
Roof / Gutters	☐	☐	☐
Fencing	☐	☐	☐

HOME SYSTEMS

	Good	Average	Poor
Electrical	☐	☐	☐
Air Conditioning / Fans	☐	☐	☐
Heating	☐	☐	☐
Security	☐	☐	☐
Plumbing	☐	☐	☐
Intercom	☐	☐	☐

FEATURES

	Good	Average	Poor
Home Warranty	☐	☐	☐
Energy Saving Features	☐	☐	☐

INTERIOR

	Good	Average	Poor
Walls / Trim / Ceilings	☐	☐	☐
Flooring	☐	☐	☐
Stairs	☐	☐	☐
Storage	☐	☐	☐
Living Room	☐	☐	☐
Family Room	☐	☐	☐
Dining Room	☐	☐	☐

	Good	Average	Poor
Master Bedroom	☐	☐	☐
Bedroom 2	☐	☐	☐
Bedroom 3	☐	☐	☐
Bedroom 4	☐	☐	☐
Master Bathroom	☐	☐	☐
Bathroom 2	☐	☐	☐
Bathroom 3	☐	☐	☐
Bonus / Game Room	☐	☐	☐

	Good	Average	Poor
Kitchen	☐	☐	☐
Cabinets	☐	☐	☐
Countertop	☐	☐	☐
Counter Space	☐	☐	☐
Flooring	☐	☐	☐
Oven / Stove	☐	☐	☐
Microwave	☐	☐	☐
Layout	☐	☐	☐
Light Fixtures	☐	☐	☐
Backsplash	☐	☐	☐
Pantry	☐	☐	☐
Appliances	☐	☐	☐
Island	☐	☐	☐

	Good	Average	Poor
Basement	☐	☐	☐
Garage	☐	☐	☐

COMMUNITY

	Good	Average	Poor
Immediate Neighborhood	☐	☐	☐
Close to Employment	☐	☐	☐
Close to Shopping	☐	☐	☐
Close to Transportation	☐	☐	☐
Close to Schools / Daycare	☐	☐	☐
Close to Places of Worship	☐	☐	☐
Near Recreational Facilities	☐	☐	☐
Close to Airport	☐	☐	☐
Near Police and Fire Department	☐	☐	☐

Address _____   Price _____

Bedrooms _____   Bathrooms _____   Sq.Ft. _____

Lot Size: _____   Year Built _____   School District _____

Annual Tax _____

EXTERIOR

	Good	Average	Poor
View/Yard/Landscaping	☐	☐	☐
Trees	☐	☐	☐
Lawn (Front)	☐	☐	☐
Lawn (Back)	☐	☐	☐
Fences (condition)	☐	☐	☐
Landscaping (condition)	☐	☐	☐
Irrigation / Sprinkler	☐	☐	☐
	☐	☐	☐
House Type	☐	☐	☐
Exterior Siding	☐	☐	☐
Deck / Patio / Porch	☐	☐	☐
Garage	☐	☐	☐
Window / Doors	☐	☐	☐
Roof / Gutters	☐	☐	☐
Fencing	☐	☐	☐

HOME SYSTEMS

	Good	Average	Poor
Electrical	☐	☐	☐
Air Conditioning / Fans	☐	☐	☐
Heating	☐	☐	☐
Security	☐	☐	☐
Plumbing	☐	☐	☐
Intercom	☐	☐	☐

FEATURES

	Good	Average	Poor
Home Warranty	☐	☐	☐
Energy Saving Features	☐	☐	☐

INTERIOR

	Good	Average	Poor
Walls / Trim / Ceilings	☐	☐	☐
Flooring	☐	☐	☐
Stairs	☐	☐	☐
Storage	☐	☐	☐
Living Room	☐	☐	☐
Family Room	☐	☐	☐
Dining Room	☐	☐	☐

	Good	Average	Poor
Master Bedroom	☐	☐	☐
Bedroom 2	☐	☐	☐
Bedroom 3	☐	☐	☐
Bedroom 4	☐	☐	☐
Master Bathroom	☐	☐	☐
Bathroom 2	☐	☐	☐
Bathroom 3	☐	☐	☐
Bonus / Game Room	☐	☐	☐

	Good	Average	Poor
Kitchen	☐	☐	☐
Cabinets	☐	☐	☐
Countertop	☐	☐	☐
Counter Space	☐	☐	☐
Flooring	☐	☐	☐
Oven / Stove	☐	☐	☐
Microwave	☐	☐	☐
Layout	☐	☐	☐
Light Fixtures	☐	☐	☐
Backsplash	☐	☐	☐
Pantry	☐	☐	☐
Appliances	☐	☐	☐
Island	☐	☐	☐

	Good	Average	Poor
Basement	☐	☐	☐
Garage	☐	☐	☐

COMMUNITY

	Good	Average	Poor
Immediate Neighborhood	☐	☐	☐
Close to Employment	☐	☐	☐
Close to Shopping	☐	☐	☐
Close to Transportation	☐	☐	☐
Close to Schools / Daycare	☐	☐	☐
Close to Places of Worship	☐	☐	☐
Near Recreational Facilities	☐	☐	☐
Close to Airport	☐	☐	☐
Near Police and Fire Department	☐	☐	☐

94

Address _____   Price _____

Bedrooms _____   Bathrooms _____   Sq.Ft. _____

Lot Size: _____   Year Built _____   School District _____

Annual Tax _____

EXTERIOR

	Good	Average	Poor
View/Yard/Landscaping	☐	☐	☐
Trees	☐	☐	☐
Lawn (Front)	☐	☐	☐
Lawn (Back)	☐	☐	☐
Fences (condition)	☐	☐	☐
Landscaping (condition)	☐	☐	☐
Irrigation / Sprinkler	☐	☐	☐
	☐	☐	☐
House Type	☐	☐	☐
Exterior Siding	☐	☐	☐
Deck / Patio / Porch	☐	☐	☐
Garage	☐	☐	☐
Window / Doors	☐	☐	☐
Roof / Gutters	☐	☐	☐
Fencing	☐	☐	☐

HOME SYSTEMS

	Good	Average	Poor
Electrical	☐	☐	☐
Air Conditioning / Fans	☐	☐	☐
Heating	☐	☐	☐
Security	☐	☐	☐
Plumbing	☐	☐	☐
Intercom	☐	☐	☐

FEATURES

	Good	Average	Poor
Home Warranty	☐	☐	☐
Energy Saving Features	☐	☐	☐

INTERIOR

	Good	Average	Poor
Walls / Trim / Ceilings	☐	☐	☐
Flooring	☐	☐	☐
Stairs	☐	☐	☐
Storage	☐	☐	☐
Living Room	☐	☐	☐
Family Room	☐	☐	☐
Dining Room	☐	☐	☐

	Good	Average	Poor
Master Bedroom	☐	☐	☐
Bedroom 2	☐	☐	☐
Bedroom 3	☐	☐	☐
Bedroom 4	☐	☐	☐
Master Bathroom	☐	☐	☐
Bathroom 2	☐	☐	☐
Bathroom 3	☐	☐	☐
Bonus / Game Room	☐	☐	☐

	Good	Average	Poor
Kitchen	☐	☐	☐
Cabinets	☐	☐	☐
Countertop	☐	☐	☐
Counter Space	☐	☐	☐
Flooring	☐	☐	☐
Oven / Stove	☐	☐	☐
Microwave	☐	☐	☐
Layout	☐	☐	☐
Light Fixtures	☐	☐	☐
Backsplash	☐	☐	☐
Pantry	☐	☐	☐
Appliances	☐	☐	☐
Island	☐	☐	☐

	Good	Average	Poor
Basement	☐	☐	☐
Garage	☐	☐	☐

COMMUNITY

	Good	Average	Poor
Immediate Neighborhood	☐	☐	☐
Close to Employment	☐	☐	☐
Close to Shopping	☐	☐	☐
Close to Transportation	☐	☐	☐
Close to Schools / Daycare	☐	☐	☐
Close to Places of Worship	☐	☐	☐
Near Recreational Facilities	☐	☐	☐
Close to Airport	☐	☐	☐
Near Police and Fire Department	☐	☐	☐

Address _____ Price _____

Bedrooms _____ Bathrooms _____ Sq.Ft. _____

Lot Size: _____ Year Built _____ School District _____

Annual Tax _____

EXTERIOR

	Good	Average	Poor
View/Yard/Landscaping	☐	☐	☐
Trees	☐	☐	☐
Lawn (Front)	☐	☐	☐
Lawn (Back)	☐	☐	☐
Fences (condition)	☐	☐	☐
Landscaping (condition)	☐	☐	☐
Irrigation / Sprinkler	☐	☐	☐
House Type	☐	☐	☐
Exterior Siding	☐	☐	☐
Deck / Patio / Porch	☐	☐	☐
Garage	☐	☐	☐
Window / Doors	☐	☐	☐
Roof / Gutters	☐	☐	☐
Fencing	☐	☐	☐

HOME SYSTEMS

	Good	Average	Poor
Electrical	☐	☐	☐
Air Conditioning / Fans	☐	☐	☐
Heating	☐	☐	☐
Security	☐	☐	☐
Plumbing	☐	☐	☐
Intercom	☐	☐	☐

FEATURES

	Good	Average	Poor
Home Warranty	☐	☐	☐
Energy Saving Features	☐	☐	☐

INTERIOR

	Good	Average	Poor
Walls / Trim / Ceilings	☐	☐	☐
Flooring	☐	☐	☐
Stairs	☐	☐	☐
Storage	☐	☐	☐
Living Room	☐	☐	☐
Family Room	☐	☐	☐
Dining Room	☐	☐	☐

	Good	Average	Poor
Master Bedroom	☐	☐	☐
Bedroom 2	☐	☐	☐
Bedroom 3	☐	☐	☐
Bedroom 4	☐	☐	☐
Master Bathroom	☐	☐	☐
Bathroom 2	☐	☐	☐
Bathroom 3	☐	☐	☐
Bonus / Game Room	☐	☐	☐

	Good	Average	Poor
Kitchen	☐	☐	☐
Cabinets	☐	☐	☐
Countertop	☐	☐	☐
Counter Space	☐	☐	☐
Flooring	☐	☐	☐
Oven / Stove	☐	☐	☐
Microwave	☐	☐	☐
Layout	☐	☐	☐
Light Fixtures	☐	☐	☐
Backsplash	☐	☐	☐
Pantry	☐	☐	☐
Appliances	☐	☐	☐
Island	☐	☐	☐

	Good	Average	Poor
Basement	☐	☐	☐
Garage	☐	☐	☐

COMMUNITY

	Good	Average	Poor
Immediate Neighborhood	☐	☐	☐
Close to Employment	☐	☐	☐
Close to Shopping	☐	☐	☐
Close to Transportation	☐	☐	☐
Close to Schools / Daycare	☐	☐	☐
Close to Places of Worship	☐	☐	☐
Near Recreational Facilities	☐	☐	☐
Close to Airport	☐	☐	☐
Near Police and Fire Department	☐	☐	☐

Address _____   Price _____

Bedrooms _____   Bathrooms _____   Sq.Ft. _____

Lot Size: _____   Year Built _____   School District _____

Annual Tax _____

EXTERIOR

	Good	Average	Poor
View/Yard/Landscaping	☐	☐	☐
Trees	☐	☐	☐
Lawn (Front)	☐	☐	☐
Lawn (Back)	☐	☐	☐
Fences (condition)	☐	☐	☐
Landscaping (condition)	☐	☐	☐
Irrigation / Sprinkler	☐	☐	☐
	☐	☐	☐
House Type	☐	☐	☐
Exterior Siding	☐	☐	☐
Deck / Patio / Porch	☐	☐	☐
Garage	☐	☐	☐
Window / Doors	☐	☐	☐
Roof / Gutters	☐	☐	☐
Fencing	☐	☐	☐

HOME SYSTEMS

	Good	Average	Poor
Electrical	☐	☐	☐
Air Conditioning / Fans	☐	☐	☐
Heating	☐	☐	☐
Security	☐	☐	☐
Plumbing	☐	☐	☐
Intercom	☐	☐	☐

FEATURES

	Good	Average	Poor
Home Warranty	☐	☐	☐
Energy Saving Features	☐	☐	☐

INTERIOR

	Good	Average	Poor
Walls / Trim / Ceilings	☐	☐	☐
Flooring	☐	☐	☐
Stairs	☐	☐	☐
Storage	☐	☐	☐
Living Room	☐	☐	☐
Family Room	☐	☐	☐
Dining Room	☐	☐	☐

	Good	Average	Poor
Master Bedroom	☐	☐	☐
Bedroom 2	☐	☐	☐
Bedroom 3	☐	☐	☐
Bedroom 4	☐	☐	☐
Master Bathroom	☐	☐	☐
Bathroom 2	☐	☐	☐
Bathroom 3	☐	☐	☐
Bonus / Game Room	☐	☐	☐

	Good	Average	Poor
Kitchen	☐	☐	☐
Cabinets	☐	☐	☐
Countertop	☐	☐	☐
Counter Space	☐	☐	☐
Flooring	☐	☐	☐
Oven / Stove	☐	☐	☐
Microwave	☐	☐	☐
Layout	☐	☐	☐
Light Fixtures	☐	☐	☐
Backsplash	☐	☐	☐
Pantry	☐	☐	☐
Appliances	☐	☐	☐
Island	☐	☐	☐

	Good	Average	Poor
Basement	☐	☐	☐
Garage	☐	☐	☐

COMMUNITY

	Good	Average	Poor
Immediate Neighborhood	☐	☐	☐
Close to Employment	☐	☐	☐
Close to Shopping	☐	☐	☐
Close to Transportation	☐	☐	☐
Close to Schools / Daycare	☐	☐	☐
Close to Places of Worship	☐	☐	☐
Near Recreational Facilities	☐	☐	☐
Close to Airport	☐	☐	☐
Near Police and Fire Department	☐	☐	☐

Address _____   Price _____

Bedrooms _____   Bathrooms _____   Sq.Ft. _____

Lot Size: _____   Year Built _____   School District _____

Annual Tax _____

EXTERIOR

	Good	Average	Poor
View/Yard/Landscaping	☐	☐	☐
Trees	☐	☐	☐
Lawn (Front)	☐	☐	☐
Lawn (Back)	☐	☐	☐
Fences (condition)	☐	☐	☐
Landscaping (condition)	☐	☐	☐
Irrigation / Sprinkler	☐	☐	☐
House Type	☐	☐	☐
Exterior Siding	☐	☐	☐
Deck / Patio / Porch	☐	☐	☐
Garage	☐	☐	☐
Window / Doors	☐	☐	☐
Roof / Gutters	☐	☐	☐
Fencing	☐	☐	☐

HOME SYSTEMS

	Good	Average	Poor
Electrical	☐	☐	☐
Air Conditioning / Fans	☐	☐	☐
Heating	☐	☐	☐
Security	☐	☐	☐
Plumbing	☐	☐	☐
Intercom	☐	☐	☐

FEATURES

	Good	Average	Poor
Home Warranty	☐	☐	☐
Energy Saving Features	☐	☐	☐

INTERIOR

	Good	Average	Poor
Walls / Trim / Ceilings	☐	☐	☐
Flooring	☐	☐	☐
Stairs	☐	☐	☐
Storage	☐	☐	☐
Living Room	☐	☐	☐
Family Room	☐	☐	☐
Dining Room	☐	☐	☐

	Good	Average	Poor
Master Bedroom	☐	☐	☐
Bedroom 2	☐	☐	☐
Bedroom 3	☐	☐	☐
Bedroom 4	☐	☐	☐
Master Bathroom	☐	☐	☐
Bathroom 2	☐	☐	☐
Bathroom 3	☐	☐	☐
Bonus / Game Room	☐	☐	☐

	Good	Average	Poor
Kitchen	☐	☐	☐
Cabinets	☐	☐	☐
Countertop	☐	☐	☐
Counter Space	☐	☐	☐
Flooring	☐	☐	☐
Oven / Stove	☐	☐	☐
Microwave	☐	☐	☐
Layout	☐	☐	☐
Light Fixtures	☐	☐	☐
Backsplash	☐	☐	☐
Pantry	☐	☐	☐
Appliances	☐	☐	☐
Island	☐	☐	☐

	Good	Average	Poor
Basement	☐	☐	☐
Garage	☐	☐	☐

COMMUNITY

	Good	Average	Poor
Immediate Neighborhood	☐	☐	☐
Close to Employment	☐	☐	☐
Close to Shopping	☐	☐	☐
Close to Transportation	☐	☐	☐
Close to Schools / Daycare	☐	☐	☐
Close to Places of Worship	☐	☐	☐
Near Recreational Facilities	☐	☐	☐
Close to Airport	☐	☐	☐
Near Police and Fire Department	☐	☐	☐

Address _____ Price _____

Bedrooms _____ Bathrooms _____ Sq.Ft. _____

Lot Size: _____ Year Built _____ School District _____

Annual Tax _____

EXTERIOR

	Good	Average	Poor
View/Yard/Landscaping	☐	☐	☐
Trees	☐	☐	☐
Lawn (Front)	☐	☐	☐
Lawn (Back)	☐	☐	☐
Fences (condition)	☐	☐	☐
Landscaping (condition)	☐	☐	☐
Irrigation / Sprinkler	☐	☐	☐
	☐	☐	☐
House Type	☐	☐	☐
Exterior Siding	☐	☐	☐
Deck / Patio / Porch	☐	☐	☐
Garage	☐	☐	☐
Window / Doors	☐	☐	☐
Roof / Gutters	☐	☐	☐
Fencing	☐	☐	☐

HOME SYSTEMS

	Good	Average	Poor
Electrical	☐	☐	☐
Air Conditioning / Fans	☐	☐	☐
Heating	☐	☐	☐
Security	☐	☐	☐
Plumbing	☐	☐	☐
Intercom	☐	☐	☐

FEATURES

	Good	Average	Poor
Home Warranty	☐	☐	☐
Energy Saving Features	☐	☐	☐

INTERIOR

	Good	Average	Poor
Walls / Trim / Ceilings	☐	☐	☐
Flooring	☐	☐	☐
Stairs	☐	☐	☐
Storage	☐	☐	☐
Living Room	☐	☐	☐
Family Room	☐	☐	☐
Dining Room	☐	☐	☐

	Good	Average	Poor
Master Bedroom	☐	☐	☐
Bedroom 2	☐	☐	☐
Bedroom 3	☐	☐	☐
Bedroom 4	☐	☐	☐
Master Bathroom	☐	☐	☐
Bathroom 2	☐	☐	☐
Bathroom 3	☐	☐	☐
Bonus / Game Room	☐	☐	☐

	Good	Average	Poor
Kitchen	☐	☐	☐
Cabinets	☐	☐	☐
Countertop	☐	☐	☐
Counter Space	☐	☐	☐
Flooring	☐	☐	☐
Oven / Stove	☐	☐	☐
Microwave	☐	☐	☐
Layout	☐	☐	☐
Light Fixtures	☐	☐	☐
Backsplash	☐	☐	☐
Pantry	☐	☐	☐
Appliances	☐	☐	☐
Island	☐	☐	☐

	Good	Average	Poor
Basement	☐	☐	☐
Garage	☐	☐	☐

COMMUNITY

	Good	Average	Poor
Immediate Neighborhood	☐	☐	☐
Close to Employment	☐	☐	☐
Close to Shopping	☐	☐	☐
Close to Transportation	☐	☐	☐
Close to Schools / Daycare	☐	☐	☐
Close to Places of Worship	☐	☐	☐
Near Recreational Facilities	☐	☐	☐
Close to Airport	☐	☐	☐
Near Police and Fire Department	☐	☐	☐

Address _____   Price _____

Bedrooms _____   Bathrooms _____   Sq.Ft. _____

Lot Size: _____   Year Built _____   School District _____

Annual Tax _____

EXTERIOR

	Good	Average	Poor
View/Yard/Landscaping	☐	☐	☐
Trees	☐	☐	☐
Lawn (Front)	☐	☐	☐
Lawn (Back)	☐	☐	☐
Fences (condition)	☐	☐	☐
Landscaping (condition)	☐	☐	☐
Irrigation / Sprinkler	☐	☐	☐
	☐	☐	☐
House Type	☐	☐	☐
Exterior Siding	☐	☐	☐
Deck / Patio / Porch	☐	☐	☐
Garage	☐	☐	☐
Window / Doors	☐	☐	☐
Roof / Gutters	☐	☐	☐
Fencing	☐	☐	☐

HOME SYSTEMS

	Good	Average	Poor
Electrical	☐	☐	☐
Air Conditioning / Fans	☐	☐	☐
Heating	☐	☐	☐
Security	☐	☐	☐
Plumbing	☐	☐	☐
Intercom	☐	☐	☐

FEATURES

	Good	Average	Poor
Home Warranty	☐	☐	☐
Energy Saving Features	☐	☐	☐

INTERIOR

	Good	Average	Poor
Walls / Trim / Ceilings	☐	☐	☐
Flooring	☐	☐	☐
Stairs	☐	☐	☐
Storage	☐	☐	☐
Living Room	☐	☐	☐
Family Room	☐	☐	☐
Dining Room	☐	☐	☐

	Good	Average	Poor
Master Bedroom	☐	☐	☐
Bedroom 2	☐	☐	☐
Bedroom 3	☐	☐	☐
Bedroom 4	☐	☐	☐
Master Bathroom	☐	☐	☐
Bathroom 2	☐	☐	☐
Bathroom 3	☐	☐	☐
Bonus / Game Room	☐	☐	☐

	Good	Average	Poor
Kitchen	☐	☐	☐
Cabinets	☐	☐	☐
Countertop	☐	☐	☐
Counter Space	☐	☐	☐
Flooring	☐	☐	☐
Oven / Stove	☐	☐	☐
Microwave	☐	☐	☐
Layout	☐	☐	☐
Light Fixtures	☐	☐	☐
Backsplash	☐	☐	☐
Pantry	☐	☐	☐
Appliances	☐	☐	☐
Island	☐	☐	☐

	Good	Average	Poor
Basement	☐	☐	☐
Garage	☐	☐	☐

COMMUNITY

	Good	Average	Poor
Immediate Neighborhood	☐	☐	☐
Close to Employment	☐	☐	☐
Close to Shopping	☐	☐	☐
Close to Transportation	☐	☐	☐
Close to Schools / Daycare	☐	☐	☐
Close to Places of Worship	☐	☐	☐
Near Recreational Facilities	☐	☐	☐
Close to Airport	☐	☐	☐
Near Police and Fire Department	☐	☐	☐

Address _____   Price _____

Bedrooms _____   Bathrooms _____   Sq.Ft. _____

Lot Size: _____   Year Built _____   School District _____

Annual Tax _____

EXTERIOR

	Good	Average	Poor
View/Yard/Landscaping	☐	☐	☐
Trees	☐	☐	☐
Lawn (Front)	☐	☐	☐
Lawn (Back)	☐	☐	☐
Fences (condition)	☐	☐	☐
Landscaping (condition)	☐	☐	☐
Irrigation / Sprinkler	☐	☐	☐
	☐	☐	☐
House Type	☐	☐	☐
Exterior Siding	☐	☐	☐
Deck / Patio / Porch	☐	☐	☐
Garage	☐	☐	☐
Window / Doors	☐	☐	☐
Roof / Gutters	☐	☐	☐
Fencing	☐	☐	☐

HOME SYSTEMS

	Good	Average	Poor
Electrical	☐	☐	☐
Air Conditioning / Fans	☐	☐	☐
Heating	☐	☐	☐
Security	☐	☐	☐
Plumbing	☐	☐	☐
Intercom	☐	☐	☐

FEATURES

	Good	Average	Poor
Home Warranty	☐	☐	☐
Energy Saving Features	☐	☐	☐

INTERIOR

	Good	Average	Poor
Walls / Trim / Ceilings	☐	☐	☐
Flooring	☐	☐	☐
Stairs	☐	☐	☐
Storage	☐	☐	☐
Living Room	☐	☐	☐
Family Room	☐	☐	☐
Dining Room	☐	☐	☐

	Good	Average	Poor
Master Bedroom	☐	☐	☐
Bedroom 2	☐	☐	☐
Bedroom 3	☐	☐	☐
Bedroom 4	☐	☐	☐
Master Bathroom	☐	☐	☐
Bathroom 2	☐	☐	☐
Bathroom 3	☐	☐	☐
Bonus / Game Room	☐	☐	☐

	Good	Average	Poor
Kitchen	☐	☐	☐
Cabinets	☐	☐	☐
Countertop	☐	☐	☐
Counter Space	☐	☐	☐
Flooring	☐	☐	☐
Oven / Stove	☐	☐	☐
Microwave	☐	☐	☐
Layout	☐	☐	☐
Light Fixtures	☐	☐	☐
Backsplash	☐	☐	☐
Pantry	☐	☐	☐
Appliances	☐	☐	☐
Island	☐	☐	☐

	Good	Average	Poor
Basement	☐	☐	☐
Garage	☐	☐	☐

COMMUNITY

	Good	Average	Poor
Immediate Neighborhood	☐	☐	☐
Close to Employment	☐	☐	☐
Close to Shopping	☐	☐	☐
Close to Transportation	☐	☐	☐
Close to Schools / Daycare	☐	☐	☐
Close to Places of Worship	☐	☐	☐
Near Recreational Facilities	☐	☐	☐
Close to Airport	☐	☐	☐
Near Police and Fire Department	☐	☐	☐

101

Address _____   Price _____

Bedrooms _____   Bathrooms _____   Sq.Ft. _____

Lot Size: _____   Year Built _____   School District _____

Annual Tax _____

EXTERIOR

	Good	Average	Poor
View/Yard/Landscaping	☐	☐	☐
Trees	☐	☐	☐
Lawn (Front)	☐	☐	☐
Lawn (Back)	☐	☐	☐
Fences (condition)	☐	☐	☐
Landscaping (condition)	☐	☐	☐
Irrigation / Sprinkler	☐	☐	☐
	☐	☐	☐
House Type	☐	☐	☐
Exterior Siding	☐	☐	☐
Deck / Patio / Porch	☐	☐	☐
Garage	☐	☐	☐
Window / Doors	☐	☐	☐
Roof / Gutters	☐	☐	☐
Fencing	☐	☐	☐

HOME SYSTEMS

	Good	Average	Poor
Electrical	☐	☐	☐
Air Conditioning / Fans	☐	☐	☐
Heating	☐	☐	☐
Security	☐	☐	☐
Plumbing	☐	☐	☐
Intercom	☐	☐	☐

FEATURES

	Good	Average	Poor
Home Warranty	☐	☐	☐
Energy Saving Features	☐	☐	☐

INTERIOR

	Good	Average	Poor
Walls / Trim / Ceilings	☐	☐	☐
Flooring	☐	☐	☐
Stairs	☐	☐	☐
Storage	☐	☐	☐
Living Room	☐	☐	☐
Family Room	☐	☐	☐
Dining Room	☐	☐	☐

	Good	Average	Poor
Master Bedroom	☐	☐	☐
Bedroom 2	☐	☐	☐
Bedroom 3	☐	☐	☐
Bedroom 4	☐	☐	☐
Master Bathroom	☐	☐	☐
Bathroom 2	☐	☐	☐
Bathroom 3	☐	☐	☐
Bonus / Game Room	☐	☐	☐

	Good	Average	Poor
Kitchen	☐	☐	☐
Cabinets	☐	☐	☐
Countertop	☐	☐	☐
Counter Space	☐	☐	☐
Flooring	☐	☐	☐
Oven / Stove	☐	☐	☐
Microwave	☐	☐	☐
Layout	☐	☐	☐
Light Fixtures	☐	☐	☐
Backsplash	☐	☐	☐
Pantry	☐	☐	☐
Appliances	☐	☐	☐
Island	☐	☐	☐

	Good	Average	Poor
Basement	☐	☐	☐
Garage	☐	☐	☐

COMMUNITY

	Good	Average	Poor
Immediate Neighborhood	☐	☐	☐
Close to Employment	☐	☐	☐
Close to Shopping	☐	☐	☐
Close to Transportation	☐	☐	☐
Close to Schools / Daycare	☐	☐	☐
Close to Places of Worship	☐	☐	☐
Near Recreational Facilities	☐	☐	☐
Close to Airport	☐	☐	☐
Near Police and Fire Department	☐	☐	☐

Address _____ Price _____

Bedrooms _____ Bathrooms _____ Sq.Ft. _____

Lot Size: _____ Year Built _____ School District _____

Annual Tax _____

EXTERIOR

	Good	Average	Poor
View/Yard/Landscaping	☐	☐	☐
Trees	☐	☐	☐
Lawn (Front)	☐	☐	☐
Lawn (Back)	☐	☐	☐
Fences (condition)	☐	☐	☐
Landscaping (condition)	☐	☐	☐
Irrigation / Sprinkler	☐	☐	☐
	☐	☐	☐
House Type	☐	☐	☐
Exterior Siding	☐	☐	☐
Deck / Patio / Porch	☐	☐	☐
Garage	☐	☐	☐
Window / Doors	☐	☐	☐
Roof / Gutters	☐	☐	☐
Fencing	☐	☐	☐

HOME SYSTEMS

	Good	Average	Poor
Electrical	☐	☐	☐
Air Conditioning / Fans	☐	☐	☐
Heating	☐	☐	☐
Security	☐	☐	☐
Plumbing	☐	☐	☐
Intercom	☐	☐	☐

FEATURES

	Good	Average	Poor
Home Warranty	☐	☐	☐
Energy Saving Features	☐	☐	☐

INTERIOR

	Good	Average	Poor
Walls / Trim / Ceilings	☐	☐	☐
Flooring	☐	☐	☐
Stairs	☐	☐	☐
Storage	☐	☐	☐
Living Room	☐	☐	☐
Family Room	☐	☐	☐
Dining Room	☐	☐	☐

	Good	Average	Poor
Master Bedroom	☐	☐	☐
Bedroom 2	☐	☐	☐
Bedroom 3	☐	☐	☐
Bedroom 4	☐	☐	☐
Master Bathroom	☐	☐	☐
Bathroom 2	☐	☐	☐
Bathroom 3	☐	☐	☐
Bonus / Game Room	☐	☐	☐

	Good	Average	Poor
Kitchen	☐	☐	☐
Cabinets	☐	☐	☐
Countertop	☐	☐	☐
Counter Space	☐	☐	☐
Flooring	☐	☐	☐
Oven / Stove	☐	☐	☐
Microwave	☐	☐	☐
Layout	☐	☐	☐
Light Fixtures	☐	☐	☐
Backsplash	☐	☐	☐
Pantry	☐	☐	☐
Appliances	☐	☐	☐
Island	☐	☐	☐

	Good	Average	Poor
Basement	☐	☐	☐
Garage	☐	☐	☐

COMMUNITY

	Good	Average	Poor
Immediate Neighborhood	☐	☐	☐
Close to Employment	☐	☐	☐
Close to Shopping	☐	☐	☐
Close to Transportation	☐	☐	☐
Close to Schools / Daycare	☐	☐	☐
Close to Places of Worship	☐	☐	☐
Near Recreational Facilities	☐	☐	☐
Close to Airport	☐	☐	☐
Near Police and Fire Department	☐	☐	☐

103

Address _____   Price _____

Bedrooms _____   Bathrooms _____   Sq.Ft. _____

Lot Size: _____   Year Built _____   School District _____

Annual Tax _____

EXTERIOR

	Good	Average	Poor
View/Yard/Landscaping	☐	☐	☐
Trees	☐	☐	☐
Lawn (Front)	☐	☐	☐
Lawn (Back)	☐	☐	☐
Fences (condition)	☐	☐	☐
Landscaping (condition)	☐	☐	☐
Irrigation / Sprinkler	☐	☐	☐
	☐	☐	☐
House Type	☐	☐	☐
Exterior Siding	☐	☐	☐
Deck / Patio / Porch	☐	☐	☐
Garage	☐	☐	☐
Window / Doors	☐	☐	☐
Roof / Gutters	☐	☐	☐
Fencing	☐	☐	☐

HOME SYSTEMS

	Good	Average	Poor
Electrical	☐	☐	☐
Air Conditioning / Fans	☐	☐	☐
Heating	☐	☐	☐
Security	☐	☐	☐
Plumbing	☐	☐	☐
Intercom	☐	☐	☐

FEATURES

	Good	Average	Poor
Home Warranty	☐	☐	☐
Energy Saving Features	☐	☐	☐

INTERIOR

	Good	Average	Poor
Walls / Trim / Ceilings	☐	☐	☐
Flooring	☐	☐	☐
Stairs	☐	☐	☐
Storage	☐	☐	☐
Living Room	☐	☐	☐
Family Room	☐	☐	☐
Dining Room	☐	☐	☐

	Good	Average	Poor
Master Bedroom	☐	☐	☐
Bedroom 2	☐	☐	☐
Bedroom 3	☐	☐	☐
Bedroom 4	☐	☐	☐
Master Bathroom	☐	☐	☐
Bathroom 2	☐	☐	☐
Bathroom 3	☐	☐	☐
Bonus / Game Room	☐	☐	☐

	Good	Average	Poor
Kitchen	☐	☐	☐
Cabinets	☐	☐	☐
Countertop	☐	☐	☐
Counter Space	☐	☐	☐
Flooring	☐	☐	☐
Oven / Stove	☐	☐	☐
Microwave	☐	☐	☐
Layout	☐	☐	☐
Light Fixtures	☐	☐	☐
Backsplash	☐	☐	☐
Pantry	☐	☐	☐
Appliances	☐	☐	☐
Island	☐	☐	☐

	Good	Average	Poor
Basement	☐	☐	☐
Garage	☐	☐	☐

COMMUNITY

	Good	Average	Poor
Immediate Neighborhood	☐	☐	☐
Close to Employment	☐	☐	☐
Close to Shopping	☐	☐	☐
Close to Transportation	☐	☐	☐
Close to Schools / Daycare	☐	☐	☐
Close to Places of Worship	☐	☐	☐
Near Recreational Facilities	☐	☐	☐
Close to Airport	☐	☐	☐
Near Police and Fire Department	☐	☐	☐

Address _____ Price _____

Bedrooms _____ Bathrooms _____ Sq.Ft. _____

Lot Size: _____ Year Built _____ School District _____

Annual Tax _____

EXTERIOR

	Good	Average	Poor
View/Yard/Landscaping	☐	☐	☐
Trees	☐	☐	☐
Lawn (Front)	☐	☐	☐
Lawn (Back)	☐	☐	☐
Fences (condition)	☐	☐	☐
Landscaping (condition)	☐	☐	☐
Irrigation / Sprinkler	☐	☐	☐
	☐	☐	☐
House Type	☐	☐	☐
Exterior Siding	☐	☐	☐
Deck / Patio / Porch	☐	☐	☐
Garage	☐	☐	☐
Window / Doors	☐	☐	☐
Roof / Gutters	☐	☐	☐
Fencing	☐	☐	☐

HOME SYSTEMS

	Good	Average	Poor
Electrical	☐	☐	☐
Air Conditioning / Fans	☐	☐	☐
Heating	☐	☐	☐
Security	☐	☐	☐
Plumbing	☐	☐	☐
Intercom	☐	☐	☐

FEATURES

	Good	Average	Poor
Home Warranty	☐	☐	☐
Energy Saving Features	☐	☐	☐

INTERIOR

	Good	Average	Poor
Walls / Trim / Ceilings	☐	☐	☐
Flooring	☐	☐	☐
Stairs	☐	☐	☐
Storage	☐	☐	☐
Living Room	☐	☐	☐
Family Room	☐	☐	☐
Dining Room	☐	☐	☐

	Good	Average	Poor
Master Bedroom	☐	☐	☐
Bedroom 2	☐	☐	☐
Bedroom 3	☐	☐	☐
Bedroom 4	☐	☐	☐
Master Bathroom	☐	☐	☐
Bathroom 2	☐	☐	☐
Bathroom 3	☐	☐	☐
Bonus / Game Room	☐	☐	☐

	Good	Average	Poor
Kitchen	☐	☐	☐
Cabinets	☐	☐	☐
Countertop	☐	☐	☐
Counter Space	☐	☐	☐
Flooring	☐	☐	☐
Oven / Stove	☐	☐	☐
Microwave	☐	☐	☐
Layout	☐	☐	☐
Light Fixtures	☐	☐	☐
Backsplash	☐	☐	☐
Pantry	☐	☐	☐
Appliances	☐	☐	☐
Island	☐	☐	☐

	Good	Average	Poor
Basement	☐	☐	☐
Garage	☐	☐	☐

COMMUNITY

	Good	Average	Poor
Immediate Neighborhood	☐	☐	☐
Close to Employment	☐	☐	☐
Close to Shopping	☐	☐	☐
Close to Transportation	☐	☐	☐
Close to Schools / Daycare	☐	☐	☐
Close to Places of Worship	☐	☐	☐
Near Recreational Facilities	☐	☐	☐
Close to Airport	☐	☐	☐
Near Police and Fire Department	☐	☐	☐

Address _____ Price _____

Bedrooms _____ Bathrooms _____ Sq.Ft. _____

Lot Size: _____ Year Built _____ School District _____

Annual Tax _____

EXTERIOR

	Good	Average	Poor
View/Yard/Landscaping	☐	☐	☐
Trees	☐	☐	☐
Lawn (Front)	☐	☐	☐
Lawn (Back)	☐	☐	☐
Fences (condition)	☐	☐	☐
Landscaping (condition)	☐	☐	☐
Irrigation / Sprinkler	☐	☐	☐
	☐	☐	☐
House Type	☐	☐	☐
Exterior Siding	☐	☐	☐
Deck / Patio / Porch	☐	☐	☐
Garage	☐	☐	☐
Window / Doors	☐	☐	☐
Roof / Gutters	☐	☐	☐
Fencing	☐	☐	☐

HOME SYSTEMS

	Good	Average	Poor
Electrical	☐	☐	☐
Air Conditioning / Fans	☐	☐	☐
Heating	☐	☐	☐
Security	☐	☐	☐
Plumbing	☐	☐	☐
Intercom	☐	☐	☐

FEATURES

	Good	Average	Poor
Home Warranty	☐	☐	☐
Energy Saving Features	☐	☐	☐

INTERIOR

	Good	Average	Poor
Walls / Trim / Ceilings	☐	☐	☐
Flooring	☐	☐	☐
Stairs	☐	☐	☐
Storage	☐	☐	☐
Living Room	☐	☐	☐
Family Room	☐	☐	☐
Dining Room	☐	☐	☐

	Good	Average	Poor
Master Bedroom	☐	☐	☐
Bedroom 2	☐	☐	☐
Bedroom 3	☐	☐	☐
Bedroom 4	☐	☐	☐
Master Bathroom	☐	☐	☐
Bathroom 2	☐	☐	☐
Bathroom 3	☐	☐	☐
Bonus / Game Room	☐	☐	☐

	Good	Average	Poor
Kitchen	☐	☐	☐
Cabinets	☐	☐	☐
Countertop	☐	☐	☐
Counter Space	☐	☐	☐
Flooring	☐	☐	☐
Oven / Stove	☐	☐	☐
Microwave	☐	☐	☐
Layout	☐	☐	☐
Light Fixtures	☐	☐	☐
Backsplash	☐	☐	☐
Pantry	☐	☐	☐
Appliances	☐	☐	☐
Island	☐	☐	☐

	Good	Average	Poor
Basement	☐	☐	☐
Garage	☐	☐	☐

COMMUNITY

	Good	Average	Poor
Immediate Neighborhood	☐	☐	☐
Close to Employment	☐	☐	☐
Close to Shopping	☐	☐	☐
Close to Transportation	☐	☐	☐
Close to Schools / Daycare	☐	☐	☐
Close to Places of Worship	☐	☐	☐
Near Recreational Facilities	☐	☐	☐
Close to Airport	☐	☐	☐
Near Police and Fire Department	☐	☐	☐

Address _____ Price _____

Bedrooms _____ Bathrooms _____ Sq.Ft. _____

Lot Size: _____ Year Built _____ School District _____

Annual Tax _____

EXTERIOR

	Good	Average	Poor
View/Yard/Landscaping	☐	☐	☐
Trees	☐	☐	☐
Lawn (Front)	☐	☐	☐
Lawn (Back)	☐	☐	☐
Fences (condition)	☐	☐	☐
Landscaping (condition)	☐	☐	☐
Irrigation / Sprinkler	☐	☐	☐
	☐	☐	☐
House Type	☐	☐	☐
Exterior Siding	☐	☐	☐
Deck / Patio / Porch	☐	☐	☐
Garage	☐	☐	☐
Window / Doors	☐	☐	☐
Roof / Gutters	☐	☐	☐
Fencing	☐	☐	☐

HOME SYSTEMS

	Good	Average	Poor
Electrical	☐	☐	☐
Air Conditioning / Fans	☐	☐	☐
Heating	☐	☐	☐
Security	☐	☐	☐
Plumbing	☐	☐	☐
Intercom	☐	☐	☐

FEATURES

	Good	Average	Poor
Home Warranty	☐	☐	☐
Energy Saving Features	☐	☐	☐

INTERIOR

	Good	Average	Poor
Walls / Trim / Ceilings	☐	☐	☐
Flooring	☐	☐	☐
Stairs	☐	☐	☐
Storage	☐	☐	☐
Living Room	☐	☐	☐
Family Room	☐	☐	☐
Dining Room	☐	☐	☐

	Good	Average	Poor
Master Bedroom	☐	☐	☐
Bedroom 2	☐	☐	☐
Bedroom 3	☐	☐	☐
Bedroom 4	☐	☐	☐
Master Bathroom	☐	☐	☐
Bathroom 2	☐	☐	☐
Bathroom 3	☐	☐	☐
Bonus / Game Room	☐	☐	☐

	Good	Average	Poor
Kitchen	☐	☐	☐
Cabinets	☐	☐	☐
Countertop	☐	☐	☐
Counter Space	☐	☐	☐
Flooring	☐	☐	☐
Oven / Stove	☐	☐	☐
Microwave	☐	☐	☐
Layout	☐	☐	☐
Light Fixtures	☐	☐	☐
Backsplash	☐	☐	☐
Pantry	☐	☐	☐
Appliances	☐	☐	☐
Island	☐	☐	☐

	Good	Average	Poor
Basement	☐	☐	☐
Garage	☐	☐	☐

COMMUNITY

	Good	Average	Poor
Immediate Neighborhood	☐	☐	☐
Close to Employment	☐	☐	☐
Close to Shopping	☐	☐	☐
Close to Transportation	☐	☐	☐
Close to Schools / Daycare	☐	☐	☐
Close to Places of Worship	☐	☐	☐
Near Recreational Facilities	☐	☐	☐
Close to Airport	☐	☐	☐
Near Police and Fire Department	☐	☐	☐

Printed in Great Britain
by Amazon

78419032R00061